Christine Chapman was brought up conviction that there is 'that of God of God's presence in all situation Anglican Church and later became a Licensed Lay Reader. present time she leads a pastoral care team in her own church.

Christine is trained as a social worker specializing in the fostering and adoption of children and has worked both for the local authority and for the Diocese of Chester's adoption service. After twelve years she felt that there was a need for greater understanding of loss and the needs of the bereaved and, after training, the Diocese's Board for Social Responsibility gave her the opportunity of training parishes in bereavement care, and going into schools which were facing the death of pupils. She also felt the need for counselling training, after which she co-ordinated a team of trained counsellors in the diocese and was later appointed Director of Counselling for twelve years.

During this time Christine wrote a book, *In Love Abiding*, responding to the needs of the bereaved, which was published by SPCK in 1995. After her retirement she joined the team of contributors for *New Daylight* and continues counselling clergy and their families for the Inter-Diocesan Counselling Service.

Christine is married with four grown-up children and eight small grandchildren from whom she has received much wisdom and guidance in how children think and feel about dying and the questions they ask.

Text copyright © Christine Chapman 2004
The author asserts the moral right
to be identified as the author of this work

Published by
The Bible Reading Fellowship
First Floor, Elsfield Hall
15–17 Elsfield Way, Oxford OX2 8FG

ISBN 1 84101 210 6
First published 2004
10 9 8 7 6 5 4 3 2 .1 0

Acknowledgments
Unless otherwise stated, scripture quotations are taken from the Contemporary
English Version of the Bible published by HarperCollins Publishers, copyright
© 1991, 1992, 1995 American Bible Society.

Scripture quotations taken from the Holy Bible, New International Version,
copyright © 1973, 1978, 1984 by International Bible Society, are used by
permission of Hodder & Stoughton Limited. All rights reserved. 'NIV' is a
registered trademark of International Bible Society. UK trademark number
1448790.

A catalogue record for this book is available from the British Library

Printed and bound in Great Britain by
Bookmarque, Croydon

SAYING GOODBYE TO GREG

UNDERSTANDING BEREAVEMENT
at Foundation, KS1 and KS2

Christine Chapman

To my grown-up children—
who shared their experiences of bereavement in schools;
who gave me their children to whom I listened and talked;
who gave me a lap-top for travelling.

To my husband—
who gave me space to write;
who acted as a sounding board, and echoed back;
who corrected mistakes with his teacher's red pen.

And to Ruth—
who guided me sensitively through guidelines
of the National Curriculum
and wrote the poem 'When Grandad died'.

ACKNOWLEDGMENTS

'Caterpillar, caterpillar' by Susan Sayers, copyright 1986 Kevin Mayhew Ltd, Buxhall, Stowmarket, Suffolk IP14 3BW. Reproduced by permission from *Hymns Old and New, Complete Anglican Edition*. Licence no. 307040

'Give me peace, O Lord' by Estelle White, copyright 1976 Kevin Mayhew Ltd, Buxhall, Stowmarket, Suffolk IP14 3BW. Reproduced by permission from *Hymns Old and New, Complete Anglican Edition*. Licence no. 307040

Extract from 'Lord of the Dance' by Sydney Carter, reproduced by permission of Stainer & Bell Ltd, London, England.

'Learning to Fly' reprinted by kind permission of Adrian Plass.

CONTENTS

FOREWORD

The pain of bereavement strikes deeply at our innermost body and soul. It leaves us powerless. The hurt is tangible and physical. You can taste it. The body throbs with pain. Emotions swirl, then divide and mix with confusion and anger. Feelings of injustice rise rapidly to the surface. The world is changed and substantially diminished. Our friend, pupil or close family member is gone—explain that if you can! The social impact alone is catastrophic.

At such a time, the spirit demands sustenance; our faith needs restoration. The knowledge that someone is thinking of us and praying for us is sympathy and condolence beyond a hundred spoken words. Adults need reassurance, comforting and understanding. Children are entitled to our informed support.

Christine Chapman gives us an insight into the ways in which one can help by providing that support. As one deeply affected by the death of my own daughter and by bereavement within my own school, I commend Christine's book to you. It's spot on.

John Hankey, Headteacher
St Thomas' CE School, Stockton Heath, Warrington, Cheshire

Chapter 1

CHILDREN'S ATTITUDES TOWARDS
THE SUBJECT OF DEATH

Most children want to talk about death. They are extremely curious about what happens when people—other people, of course—die. They want to ask lots of questions: 'Where is heaven, if it's not in the sky? What happens to your body when it's buried? Who'll look after me when you die?'

Adults, on the other hand, do not usually want to talk about death. It reminds us of our own mortality. It brings up pain from our own bereavements and it makes us feel ignorant because we do not know all the answers. Yet we avoid the subject at our children's cost. They soon get the message that it is not all right to talk about this very interesting subject with grown-ups, so they leap to their own, often bizarre, conclusions. They keep their anxieties to themselves, and they do not learn how to cope with themselves or others when, sooner or later, death comes their way.

We adults may like to kid ourselves that children do not grieve anyway, or that they are resilient and soon 'get over it'. We want to protect them from suffering during their childhood at least, and keep the world a happy place with happy endings. But in fact, children do grieve for relations, friends and pets who die. They go through a similar grief process as adults, but they do not have the words to express it, the experience to understand it, or the emotional stamina to sustain it. It comes in bursts between normal happy activities. It comes as aggression, regression, frustration, or tears over something quite trivial. So we respond inappropriately, and leave children feeling angry, misunderstood and confused.

Teachers, in particular, may find it hard to face children's questions about death. What does happen when people die—exactly? We do not know all the answers. But teachers are expected to know everything and, furthermore, what they say goes. If death breaks into a school suddenly, teachers are expected to extend their capabilities far beyond their normal expertise, keep themselves together in the midst of overwhelming emotions and respond to the children's urgent needs as well as they can—in addition to maintaining the momentum of the school day.

There are guidelines for understanding the grief process of children, recognizing the symptoms they show and responding in the most helpful way. If we look at these guidelines and at how we can apply them, and if we are prepared to open ourselves to the vulnerabilities that death brings to the surface, then we have the key to responding to the very real needs of children who are bereaved. We can unlock the healing of their hurts, the growth that comes from facing their pain, the freedom to learn new skills and develop fuller potential, and the confidence to face life and death with more understanding and less fear.

This and the following chapters describe a real-life situation, in story form, in which a school faced and dealt with the death of one of their children. The characters in the story are fictitious, but the situation portrayed can be used as a basis for learning and discussion.

Let me introduce you to Margaret, the headteacher of Hillside Primary School.

FIRST REACTIONS—AND ACTIONS

She was sitting by the phone, frozen with shock, trying to think what she should do. It had been the worst day of her life since she had started teaching. Nothing in her pastoral care training had prepared her for this. She kept hearing the chilling words of the policewoman who had phoned earlier that evening: 'I'm sorry to have to tell you that one of the children from your school has had a fatal accident.'

'You mean…?'

'Gregory Mitchell. He was killed instantly this evening when he lost control of his roller-blades and was knocked down by a car…'

THE HEAD: GETTING IT RIGHT FOR THE CHILDREN AND THE STAFF

Margaret felt as if a block of ice was between her and the rest of the world. She sat for a while and then rang the police station back just to make sure she had heard aright, and to ask questions. Then she sank down on a chair to try to think clearly about what she should do. She had been headmistress for only a term and was trying so hard to get everything right. How would the teachers cope with this? They needed to be prepared, now, and she would have to let them know. She took a deep breath and telephoned the other members of staff, then the teaching and lunchtime assistants. Repeating the same words over and over again helped to make it more real for her, but then she had to deal with their reactions. Greg's class teacher, Carole, was the hardest. She did not seem to accept it at all. Margaret arranged to meet Carole at eight o'clock next morning in her classroom.

Then she phoned Oliver MacKenzie, the vicar, who came occasionally to take Assembly. After asking a few questions, he said quietly, 'Is there anything I can do to help you?'

Margaret thought about the next day. 'Could you come and do an Assembly tomorrow and say some prayers?'

'Of course,' he agreed, and then added quietly, 'I'll be praying for you, too.'

Margaret put the phone down and wept. She had always thought she had some kind of faith, but when she thought of God now she felt bewildered, and suddenly angry. Why hadn't God stopped the accident? Why couldn't he have delayed the car for a few seconds?

And where was he now? She felt she did not know anything for certain any more. Then she thought of the children. How would they feel? How would they react? She resolved there and then that Hillside Primary School—her school—must provide a safe, comforting, caring environment for all the children, and especially for Gareth and Ellie, Greg's brother and sister. They must have opportunities to ask questions and express their feelings in some way. She hoped the teachers would understand this.

THE STAFF: GREG'S TEACHER

Margaret arrived at school before eight the next morning and went straight to Greg's classroom. Carole was already there, looking pale and tight-lipped, moving chairs and tables around very noisily and arranging some cushions on the floor. She hardly looked up as Margaret came in. 'Don't ask me to take lessons this morning. I don't know how we're going to cope. I can't bear to look at his work on the wall, or his books or PE kit hanging on the peg. And there's his empty place at that table.'

It was all too awful for words and Margaret could only think how *young* Carole looked. How could she offer Carole the necessary support without the kind of sympathy that would break her down? She hoped she sounded calmer and more confident than she felt. 'Take as much time as you need to talk with the children and answer their questions.'

She glanced round the room and saw Greg's name in bold blue print on his drawer, and a picture of a castle on the wall with his name on it. 'Leave his work up, and his place empty for the moment and let the children decide what they want to do with them. And Carole, you might consider going to see Greg's mum and dad in the next day or two and asking them what they would like us to do with his things. I'll come with you,' she added quickly, seeing the look of fear on Carole's face.

'I couldn't do that,' said Carole. 'See Greg's mum, I mean. I wouldn't know what to say. He was always so careful on his roller-blades. I know. I've seen him. He's brilliant. He… was… brilliant.'

'I know.'

'I just wish I could protect the children and tell them everything will be all right.'

'I wish that, too,' said Margaret. 'But there will be a lot of things about Greg's death that will make them anxious and afraid and we need to take their feelings seriously and be ready to answer any questions they want to ask. Otherwise their fears will stay buried deep down and they will be there whenever they have to cope with death in the future. It's terribly important that we get it right for them now and don't just get on with lessons as usual.'

'I just hope I can do it,' said Carole tearfully. 'But I've never had to do anything like this before.'

'You are doing all the right things,' said Margaret looking round at the informal arrangement of cushions on the floor. 'Come along to the staff room now, Carole, we need to talk about these things all together.'

STAFF MEETING

The other teachers were unusually quiet as Margaret and Carole went into the staff room.

'Good morning,' said Margaret. 'I just want to tell you not to worry about keeping to normal lessons this morning. We need to give time for the children who knew Greg well to try to say goodbye to him in whatever way seems appropriate to them, and to let them say what is on their minds, what they are feeling, and to ask any questions. Some of their parents will be willing to listen and answer questions but others won't, or won't be able to. I see the role of teachers as really important in this. We're not just here to teach the National Curriculum. We're here to prepare the children in our care for life—and death when it happens.

'I'm going to ask the school secretary to buy a book and a candle and some flowers and I'll set up a table in the hall for anyone—children, teachers, assistants, parents—anyone who knew Greg to write just a sentence about what they liked about him, or some contact they had with him. We'll try to find a good photograph of him too. I will be there this lunchtime, and after school each day this week if I can, but I'd like one of you to take over when I can't be there. I'll be writing a letter to parents to tell them exactly what happened, and how we're dealing with it, and to let them know about the book. I don't know when Ellie and Gareth will be back'—she turned to Lorraine who took Foundation and Alan who had Year 6—'but you might like to prepare the children for that and ask them if there is anything they would like to do for Ellie or Gareth.

'I suggest that you spend the next forty minutes telling your classes clearly what happened as far as we know, so that any false stories are straightened out, and then give them time to respond. Children sometimes have all kinds of misconceptions about death, as well as fears and worries, and if they aren't dealt with at the time they stay in their minds as they grow up. We'll have a special Assembly after you have talked with your classes. I've asked the vicar to come.

'I'll leave it to you how you spend the rest of the day. Greg's class may want to think of ways of saying goodbye to him, and Gareth and Ellie's classes may have things they would like to do. All the children will have questions they need to ask. Take it from them, but keep some lesson structure for part of the day if you can. Some routine is important for their sense of security.'

Margaret paused and then went on, 'I do appreciate how difficult it is, especially for those who have taught Greg. You have got your own feelings to deal with as well as responding to the children's questions. I would advise you to answer only what they ask, and no more, and to try to be truthful. Don't be afraid to say you don't know, but say it with confidence. And—I just want you to know that I'm here to support you in any way that I can. Is there anything anyone would like to say?'

'Yes.' Frances, the teacher of Year 4, spoke up. 'My class need to get on with lessons as usual. We're not closely involved with Greg and it's all we can do to keep up with the National Curriculum.'

'I know,' said Margaret, 'but please give them a chance to talk over how they are feeling. We don't know what's in their minds. Besides, if the children are worried or upset, they won't be able to work anyway.'

'I can't agree with you.' Frances stood her ground. 'Unfortunately Greg has died and there's nothing anyone can do about it. Talking won't bring him back. What children need when something like this happens is routine and security—things going on as usual. I'm sure the previous Head would have felt the same. She was very concerned about the position of our school in the league tables.'

Margaret winced inwardly. She was sure of her ground when talking about pastoral care, but not nearly so confident about her authority as Head.

Frances went on, 'I know. My mother died when I was about the same age as Gareth, and I really needed the structure and routine of school to stop me thinking about it all the time.'

So that was it. Margaret felt sympathy for Frances but was all the more determined to allow the children the opportunity to air their feelings now, as they came up. She looked out of the window and saw the playground filling with children.

'We'll have to finish now. I'm still going to ask all of you to give some time to talking with your classes about Greg, and about death generally if the children voice concerns about it. I'll come round and see how you're getting on. Bring your classes in now instead of waiting for the bell, and we'll have Assembly at quarter to ten.'

Despite Margaret's firmness, Frances had cast some doubts into her mind and she decided to ring the Education Offices to ask for advice. She was eventually put through to a schools' counsellor who said she had some experience in dealing with bereavement in schools. She was called Adele, and she offered to come to the school at the end of that day. 'Usually, in a primary school, the teachers are the best ones to cope with their children,' she said, 'because they know the children and the children trust them. But the teachers themselves will need support, and they might be glad to unload at the end of the day.'

THE CHILDREN: QUESTIONS AND ANSWERS

FOUNDATION

Some of the children had heard about Greg, but not all. Lorraine found it particularly difficult with her Foundation class. After she had explained what had happened and how Ellie might be away for a few days, they still asked whether Greg would come back next week or next year. Lorraine tried hard to answer just what the children asked—and to be truthful.

'Greg won't be back next week or next year. He has died and he can't come back.'

'My Nan says you become a star in the sky when you die.'

'Does she?' Lorraine thought for a moment. She did not like to challenge Nan's authority on the subject, but where did the truth come in? 'That's a nice thing to say, but stars are stars and Greg is... well, Greg, but in heaven.'

'Is heaven in the sky?'

'No, heaven is not in the sky.' Lorraine spoke with more confidence now. 'Heaven is where God and Jesus live.'

'But Jesus lives in the sky. It says so in "Away in a manger".'

So it did. Some hymns had a lot to answer for.

'Is heaven above the sky?'

Lorraine felt suddenly weary and remembered what Margaret had said about admitting when you don't know.

'We don't really know where heaven is. But we will one day.'

'I saw Greg last night.' Lorraine looked at the girl who had spoken. She was Ellie's friend, Hollie.

'No, dear, you couldn't have seen him. Greg died in the afternoon.'

'I did. I saw him with a man. They were talking.' Lorraine thought she had better not argue with this one, but she did ask, 'What did they look like, Hollie?'

Hollie thought. 'The man was really nice. Greg had his green school sweatshirt on.'

'Yes, well… what were you going to say, Jack?'

'Will Ellie be able to play with Greg's scooter now? Or has Greg taken it with him?'

'Greg won't need his scooter now. Ellie will be able to play with it if her mum says it's all right.'

Lorraine felt it was all a bit unreal. As for Hollie, had she really 'seen' Greg or was she making it up? She was not the kind of child who made things up. She breathed a sigh of relief when the bell rang for Assembly.

YEAR 3: GREG'S CLASS

The children in Greg's class were silent and tearful. His presence was missed. His drawing was on the wall. His name was on his drawer and his PE kit was on the peg. Worse still, his place at the table was empty. Carole told the children to sit down with her on the cushions in the 'comfy corner' she had created. There was a large box of tissues by her side. She went over what had happened yesterday afternoon after Greg had left school. 'He would not have felt pain; apparently he died immediately.'

Some of the children wept quietly while Greg's friend Abby began to sob. Carole felt suddenly that she was going to cry and shared out the tissues. She was glad that Joan, the teaching assistant, was with her. 'We're going to have to comfort each other,' she told them. 'It's all right to cry, and it's all right to comfort each other.'

They talked about Greg's work on the wall, and his name on his drawer. 'Do you want to take them away, or leave them where are for the moment?' she asked.

'Don't take them down,' said Abby.

'What would you like to do with them?' asked Carole.

'Perhaps we could keep his name because he's in our class,' said one girl. 'But then we could give the other things to his mum and dad.'

Carole asked them if they would like to make a card for Ellie, or for Greg's mum and dad. 'We could make a big card together and I'll take it to them.'

'Could I make a special card?' asked Abby, and started to sob again, setting some of the others off too. Joan went over and put her hand on Abby's shoulder and Abby almost shouted, 'Don't let them put him in a box. My grandad was put in a box.'

Carole tried to speak reasonably. 'Abby, Greg's body will lie in a case that has been made specially for him.'

'What if he wakes up? Grandad's box was shut.'

❖

Carole looked round in panic and saw that Margaret had come into the classroom and was sitting quietly at the back. How long had she been there? Margaret motioned to her to go on and Carole tried her best with Abby. 'His body couldn't wake up, because it's dead. The doctors make quite sure of that. He can't feel anything, or see or hear. He can't breathe. He's dead.'

'Well, how can he go to heaven then? Will he be able to open up the box and get out?'

Carole took courage from Margaret's presence. 'No, it's not like that. Greg's spirit—that's the real Greg—left his body when he died and went to heaven.'

There was a silence while the children, and Carole, who did not know she had it in her, tried to digest all this. Then Abby said quietly, 'He will have friends in heaven, won't he?'

'Yes, he will have lots of friends because everyone is friends in heaven. And Jesus will look after him too.'

Never was Carole so glad to hear the bell for the end of the session. As the children filed out of the room, Margaret touched her arm. 'Well done! Just think how terrified Abby was, knowing so much, but never having it explained to her.'

YEAR 6

Gareth's class in Year 6 was subdued. Gareth was one of the quieter ones, but they missed him. When Alan, their teacher, asked them how they thought Gareth might be feeling, his friend Mike said, 'Gareth will be very, very sad and he'll be crying. And he doesn't like anyone to see him crying so he'll be in his bedroom. Couldn't we bring him here?'

'We can't do that,' said Alan, 'but why don't you ask your mum if Gareth could come and play at your house one day after school this week. He does come sometimes, doesn't he?'

'He often comes,' said Mike. 'We usually go roller-blading... oh...' His voice trailed off. 'I can't think why Greg went on the road. His dad always told us to keep on the pavements.'

Alan tried to explain that Greg must have lost control. The children were plainly unnerved by this. 'I don't think I want to ride my bike any more,' said one. 'The brakes might not work.'

'Look,' said Alan, 'you must go on roller-blading and cycling. It's part of your lives. If we never took risks, life would not be worth living and you would not achieve anything. It's dangerous every time you cross the road, but you all look both ways carefully, don't you? What happened to Greg was very, very unlucky and very, very unusual but I don't think he would have wanted to stay in all the time and not do exciting things, do you?' They weren't sure. Some of them agreed. Alan could see he needed to take this up with them again later.

❖

'Perhaps we could make a quiet corner over there,' said Alan. 'Then when Gareth comes back he can go and read a book or just be quiet if he needs to—and so could any of you,' he added. 'My guess is that Gareth will want to seem like everyone else and play as usual, most of the time. But he might want to be on his own too sometimes.'

'There's the football match on Friday,' said Mike. 'Gareth won't want to miss out on that.'

'If any of you would like to write a letter to him, I think he would be very pleased,' said Alan.

'What do we say?' asked Tom, the football team captain.

'Tell him how upset we all were to hear about Greg,' said Alan. 'And then perhaps you could say something nice you remember about him. And you could mention that you'll miss Gareth on the team and hope he will come back as soon as he can.'

The children and their teachers were glad when the time for Assembly came. It seemed like normal, except that everyone was quiet.

CHECKPOINTS

- Accept that children do grieve, but in a different way from adults.
- Take stock of your own attitude towards dying; overcome any reluctance to admit that you do not know all the answers.
- Inform all the staff about what has happened. Ask classroom assistants to go to those classes where they will be most needed.
- Consider creating a place, or 'bolt-hole', where children might go when upset.
- Explain clearly and unambiguously to the children the events leading up to the death.
- Set aside the time to answer children's questions, and to listen to their thoughts and feelings. Answer only what they ask, and try to be as truthful as possible.
- Encourage the children to comfort each other.
- Consider the role that a clergyperson might take.

- Acknowledge the need for teachers to have a support network from outside school.
- Consider having a book of remembrance for adults and children to write in.

Chapter 2

WHEN A SCHOOL IS BEREAVED

A family is usually shaken to the core by the death of one of its close members. Its whole structure changes, its behaviour patterns become unpredictable and the familiar supports break down. The family is no longer a place of safety and security for its children.

A school, on the other hand, will not usually be shaken to the core by the death of one of its members. It may tremble, but its structure and support systems should remain in place. With understanding and flexibility within the normal routine, a primary school can provide a safe, stable and, we would hope, loving environment in which little ones suffering from bereavement can find their new feet, and gain confidence to continue their development and concentrate on their learning again.

The structure of a school does not just happen, however. The headteacher and staff provide the supports and if they too are trembling from bereavement they will need extra support, perhaps from an outside agency, to enable them to cope with the needs of their children. They may welcome this support at the end of the day, before they go home to face families or partners or to be on their own.

So what are the needs of children in the classroom after a death has occurred? We have already mentioned the need to allow space to respond to questions, and to explain clearly how the death occurred at the level the children can understand, but that is not enough. Children also need help in identifying their feelings and expressing them. They need to be aware of what this particular bereavement means to them—what the person meant to them— and they need to try to complete in some way any unfinished business that remains between them and the one who has died.

Children also need to take a break from this emotionally exhausting work, to laugh and shout and play as normal. Again, the school provides natural outlets for this in playtimes and lunch breaks, PE, craft and music activities.

Teachers can encourage the children to comfort each other and to feel supported by the class. They need to know too when to return to routine lessons and normal discipline, so that the children know that the world is still going on and still has some predictability and security.

Much is expected of teachers at all times, and especially at times of bereavement. Teachers in primary schools have a unique relationship with their children, and usually a good understanding of their individual needs.

Let us return to Hillside Primary School to see how its teachers are coping with the rest of the day.

ASSEMBLY

Assembly seemed like normal except that the vicar was there and he only came occasionally. Margaret greeted the children as usual and said that she knew many of them would be feeling very shocked and very sad because Greg had died. 'Your teachers will help you to think of your own ways of saying goodbye to him. Miss Williams and I are going to see Greg's mum and dad tomorrow and if any of you want to make a card for Gareth and Ellie we'll take it along. Later in the week we'll talk about what else we can do. But now we'll start assembly with a hymn and then Mr MacKenzie will lead us in prayer.'

Frances played the first line of 'He's got the whole world in his hands' more quietly and thoughtfully than she usually played it. The children started to sing and got louder as the verses went on. Margaret sensed a togetherness and strengthening of spirits through the singing and suggested that for the last verse they sang, 'He's got our friend, Greg, in his hands.'

Then the vicar came forward. He said, 'I'm going to pray to Jesus now. If you don't pray to Jesus you might like to say God's name instead. Or you could just sit quietly and think of Greg. All right?' The children sat down and bowed their heads as Oliver MacKenzie began.

'Jesus, you are our friend in heaven. We know you love all of us, and especially Greg. We thank you for Greg—what he was to his friends and his class and his teachers. Be with us as we miss him and think about him. Please help us today to begin to say our goodbyes to him. Bless Gareth and Ellie and their mum and dad. Help them to bear this with you and to entrust Greg into your care. Help us also to trust you, Lord Jesus, for you are our friend on earth and now Greg's friend in heaven. Amen.

'And now let's say together the prayer that Jesus taught us: Our Father...'

The children joined in, again beginning quietly and gaining confidence as they said the prayer together. Then the vicar lifted his hands and concluded, 'May the blessing of God be upon you all, especially those who were close to Greg, now and always. Amen.

'One last thing.' The children looked up. 'Some of you may be feeling that there are things you would have liked to say to Greg if he were here today, or things you would have liked to do. Or you may have quarrelled with him and be feeling bad because you can't put it right with him. Well, don't think it's too late. Tell Jesus about it and ask him to make things right between you and Greg. Or write a letter to him and we'll offer it to God. Think of Jesus as the one who is looking after Greg—and caring for you too.'

Margaret was surprised to hear that. But Greg did pick fights sometimes and he had not been above teasing some of the girls. There may well be some children feeling bad or with some un-finished business to sort out. And if Jesus is here for us, and also there more fully for those who have died, then it made sense to pray to him.

A BOOK FOR GREG

After another hymn, the children went out into the playground and Margaret went into her office. Janet, the school secretary, was there with a beautiful loose-leafed book, a large white candle she had bought and some primroses she had picked. She had also found a recent photograph of Greg, gap-toothed and smiling. She helped Margaret to find a small table and a vase, and together they placed the book in the middle of the table and the photograph, flowers and candle behind it.

Margaret lit the candle, sat down at the table and wrote on the inside cover: 'This book is about Gregory Mitchell, written by those who knew him and miss him.' Then, on the first page she wrote, 'Greg was part of all our lives at Hillside School for three and a half years. He was full of joy, had a strong sense of adventure and many friends. Greg made his mark at school. His short life was not in vain.'

HELPING THE CHILDREN IN THEIR GRIEF

YEAR 3: THINKING ABOUT GREG

Acting on Margaret's advice, Carole spent playtime putting three big sheets of paper up on the wall. On the first she wrote, 'Thoughts about Greg.' On the second she wrote, 'Feelings about Greg.' And on the third sheet of paper she wrote, 'Unfinished business with Greg.' Then she put various coloured sheets of paper and card out on the tables and got out paints, felt-tips, and modelling and craft materials.

When the children came in from playtime, Carole told them to sit down among the cushions. Then she pointed to the first sheet. 'Let's all think about Greg for a minute. What kind of a person was he? Start by calling out any word that comes into your head when you think of him.'

There was a silence as the children looked at the blank piece of paper. Then Carole wrote 'happy' and 'good fun'. The children began to voice their thoughts.

'Greg shared his pens with me when I'd forgotten mine.'

'Yes, he always shared his crisps.'

Carole wrote 'sharing'.

'He was very quick at his work and didn't mind anyone copying.'

'That was because he didn't always get it right,' said Carole, trying to get them to laugh a bit. She wrote 'generous'.

'Kind.'

'Never mean.'

'Good at football.'

'Good at burping,' shouted out one boy and everyone laughed, and went on laughing longer than normal.

When they were serious again, Carole asked, 'Was there anything you didn't like about Greg? He wasn't always good, any more than the rest of us. He was a bit cheeky to me sometimes.' She wrote, 'Cheeky at times.'

'He laughed at me when I fell and hurt myself in the playground.'

'He hid my lunchbox, just for a joke.'

Carole wrote, 'Sometimes a bit unkind.'

'He may not have been good all the time,' burst out Abby, 'but he was my very best friend and he was always nice to me.'

'A good friend.'

YEAR 3: FEELINGS ABOUT GREG

Carole pointed to the second sheet of paper. 'What about "feelings"? What we feel is very real and very important to us. Abby, I know this is hard, but could you try to say what you feel like when you think of Greg?'

'I don't know, I just hurt and hurt all over,' sobbed Abby. Carole went over and knelt down beside her. 'Sometimes it helps a bit if you paint what it's like, hurting so much. Would you like to try to do that?' Abby nodded miserably. As Carole knew, she liked painting.

'Jess, would you go with Abby? And anyone else who would like to paint or model what it feels like to hurt, go and join Jess and Abby at that table. Mrs Critchley will go with you.' She turned to the others. 'Now, can anyone else say how they are feeling?'

There was a silence. Carole tried to help them. 'I think I feel sad… and a bit angry… and I can't think properly. Does anyone else feel like that?'

'I'm scared,' said one girl.

'So am I,' said another. 'It's not nice any more.'

'I can understand that,' said Carole. 'Is there anything you'd like to do about feeling scared?

The girl thought and eventually said, 'I'd like to go and hide somewhere.'

'We could make a den.'

'I want to make a cave out of clay.'

'Good idea,' said Carole. 'All the paints and modelling and craft things are out. And you could make a den in that corner.' Joan set up a corner of the classroom and started some more children off on activities.

'Does anyone else feel angry?' asked Carole. 'I feel like shaking my fists. It shouldn't have happened.'

'You could growl,' suggested one boy. 'Like this—Grrrrrrr……'

❖

Carole worked hard on feelings, but the children seemed unable to say how they felt. They did settle down to writing poems and making pictures of Greg, though. She decided to leave the 'feelings' sheet of paper up on the wall and go back to it later.

YEAR 3: DEALING WITH UNFINISHED BUSINESS

Later that morning, after attempting unsuccessfully to do some work with the children, Carole pointed to the sheet of paper with

'Unfinished business' on it. 'Is anyone left with things they should have done or said to Greg? Or anything you feel bad about?'

'He lent me 20p to buy sweets on the way home yesterday,' said one girl, 'and now I can't give it him back.'

'I wonder what you could do with that 20p,' asked Carole.

The girl thought for a minute. 'I could buy some sweets for Ellie.'

'Yes, you could,' said Carole. 'I think Ellie will be back at school later this week.'

'I used to fight with Greg a lot,' said Jack, 'and I'd get him into trouble by saying he started it. I pretended he hurt me really badly once when he didn't. I wish I hadn't done that.'

'Didn't you and Greg like each other much?' asked Carole sympathetically.

'Not really. But you know what the vicar said…'

'Yes. Could you talk to Jesus about it, Jack?'

'No. Wouldn't know what to say.'

'Could you write a letter to Jesus?'

'Dad says there isn't a Jesus or God. I could write a letter to the vicar and tell him not to read it.'

Carole was a little uncertain about Jack's theology but felt somehow that he had got it right for himself.

❖

Abby's picture of a girl, presumably herself, with a splodge of red paint in the stomach area and red and black streaks coming out of her face and hands, made Carole feel unsteady again.

'That must be how Greg's mum and dad are feeling, too.'

'Shall we give it them?' asked Abby.

'How about cutting it out and sticking it on to a card and asking if anyone would like to sign it?' asked Carole. 'Then we could send it from all of us.'

'I'll cut it out,' said Jess. 'Come on Abby,' and the two girls settled down quite happily again.

❖

After lunch, Year 3 had ordinary lessons. Carole felt that some routine was necessary for the children's security. Their emotional stamina was exhausted for the present—to say nothing of hers. She finished the day by getting out her guitar and having a class sing-along.

FOUNDATION: UNDERSTANDING THE CHANGES
BROUGHT ABOUT BY DEATH

Lorraine's class had stories. Lorraine liked telling stories and the children seemed particularly fascinated by the story of the caterpillar that turned into a butterfly. She had the children crawling about on their tummies as caterpillars, curling up in a ball and going to sleep in a pretend chrysalis. Then, when she clapped suddenly and loudly, they leapt up as butterflies and flew round the classroom. She told them that it was a bit like that with Greg. When he was with them he had a body like they had, with legs and arms and a head which he needed to live in this world. But now he had died, God would give him another body which was right for his new life in heaven.

'Can Greg fly now?'

'Has he got lots of colours all over?'

'No, Greg isn't a butterfly. He will have a different kind of body, but we don't quite know what it is like.' Lorraine felt a bit out of her depth. It was a feeling most of the teachers experienced in the days to come. They almost got used to it. They could only answer the children's questions so far, and they learned to say with confidence that they did not know exactly.

❖

Lorraine returned to normal lessons before the end of the morning, feeling that a bit of normality was in order for her sake as well as the children's. In the afternoon she spoke to them about Ellie. 'We don't know when Ellie will be coming back,' she said, 'but it might be tomorrow. Do you think we can look after her?'

YEAR 6: THINKING ABOUT GREG'S BROTHER; CONCERNS ABOUT THE DANGERS OF LIFE

Gareth's class were restless. Some of them had known Greg well through going to Gareth's house. They felt miserable for Gareth. Alan, their teacher, felt miserable too. He liked Gareth and he hated to think of him being upset. He felt he needed to take some initiative now to help settle the children—and himself too. 'What do you think of the idea of making a big collage on the wall of the things you've seen Gareth doing with Greg—or things you've seen Greg doing? We could give it to Gareth as our tribute to Greg.'

'Yes, can we do one about Greg at school and one at home?' said Mike, Gareth's friend. 'But we can't do one of him roller-blading, can we?'

'Perhaps not, just now,' said Alan. 'But we can't ignore Greg's roller-blading,' he continued, seeing his opportunity to tackle the subject again. 'He had lots of fun with his roller-blades and I understand that he was really good on them.'

'Why did he die, then?'

'As I told you before, he came off the pavement on to the road just as a car was passing. It wasn't like him at all.'

'Did it hurt?'

'I don't think Greg even saw the car,' said Alan. 'It all happened so quickly.'

'But he might have seen it and felt terrified, and then felt a big bang.'

'That is possible. We can only hope it wasn't like that.'

'Is it always dangerous, roller-blading?'

'Look,' said Alan, 'it's all about being careful whether you're cycling, roller-blading or skateboarding. It can be dangerous, but it's also exciting and fun.'

'Greg liked doing exciting things. He wouldn't have been Greg if he didn't,' said Mike.

'Exactly. Now let's get on with our collage.'

❖

'Can I do one of Gareth and Greg playing football?'

'Can I draw Greg at the disco?'

Alan sent one of the children out to the storeroom for materials, because his class did not often do collages these days. He suggested that some of them worked in pairs on backgrounds—the school playground, the park, the hall where the disco had taken place. The children talked as they worked, about Greg, about Gareth, and about people they knew who had died. They spent most of the morning working on the collage, and when Margaret came in to see how they were doing, she found the whole of one wall full of Greg and Gareth.

THE END OF THE DAY

Margaret called a short staff meeting at the end of the day to introduce Adele, the bereavement counsellor, who had offered to come in that afternoon. 'I'm here to support you in any way I can,' she said. 'You must have had a very difficult and exhausting day with the children, and now you have to go home and deal with your own situations. I'll be here every day this week after school if you want to talk or ask questions.' Margaret then thanked the teachers for responding to their children in such a sensitive, caring way when they too were upset. No one seemed to want to talk. They were too tired and upset.

VISIT TO GREG'S PARENTS

It was with considerable reluctance that Carole agreed to go with Margaret to see Greg's parents the following day. 'I'd really rather not. I wouldn't know what to say,' she protested.

'It's not about knowing what to say,' said Margaret. 'It's about letting them know that we, Greg's teachers, care terribly about what's happened. It's about sharing in their grief in a very small way.'

'But won't that make it worse? Grief is awful, it's horrible.'

'Yes, but if it's so awful for us, think what it's like for the parents,' said Margaret grimly. 'Please come if you possibly can, Carole. It will mean a lot to them to see you, Greg's teacher. Perhaps you could look out some of his work, and his PE kit.'

'Well... some of the class made a card for them. I could bring that, too.'

'It will be easier to go with something in our hands,' said Margaret. She was finding it difficult too. The thought of witnessing the parents' grief was unbearable, but she knew she had to do it.

❖

They drove the short distance to Greg's house in silence, Carole clutching the bag with Greg's things in it and Margaret clutching the steering wheel as if it were her stomach. The door was opened by a woman they did not know.

'We're from Greg's school,' said Margaret quietly. 'I'm Margaret Norbury, the headteacher, and this is Carole Williams, Greg's teacher. We just wanted to say how devastated we all are...' Margaret stopped. She couldn't think of the right words. Perhaps there weren't any.

'I'm Greg's aunt,' said the woman. 'I'll see if Sue wants to see you.' She disappeared and Carole whispered, 'I feel like running away.' But the aunt returned. 'Do come in,' she said pleasantly, and showed them into the living-room where Sue Mitchell was standing staring out of the window.

'Mrs Mitchell, we had to come. The whole school is shocked and grief-stricken,' began Margaret. Sue Mitchell turned round and the sight of her face brought Carole suddenly to life. Unable to stop her tears, she said impulsively, 'Mrs Mitchell, we're going to miss Greg so much. I can't imagine what it's like for you.' Margaret watched as the two women put their arms round each other. She wished she could be as emotionally open as Carole. Actions spoke far more than words.

❖

Neil Mitchell had come into the room. 'It's good of you to come,' he said. 'You must know Greg pretty well.'

'We all loved Greg,' said Margaret. 'His class have sent you a card. Abby made it. She was quite inconsolable.'

Carole got out the card and Neil thanked her. 'I expect you knew things about Greg that even we didn't know.'

'Is there anything else you would like just now?' asked Margaret. 'His schoolwork, or his PE clothes?'

'Have you got his clothes?' asked Sue, speaking for the first time. Carole got out Greg's shoebag and Sue picked out his shirt and shorts and buried her face in them, sobbing uncontrollably. Neil went over to her and Margaret said quietly, 'We'll be going now,' and steered Carole out of the room. The aunt met them in the hall. 'Ellie and Gareth are with my other sister. Ellie might be best coming back to school tomorrow.'

❖

Not till she was home in her flat did Margaret put her head in her hands and let the tears come. She had no husband at home to talk to and she felt suddenly desolate. She kept seeing Greg's laughing face as he had left school only two days before. She thought of an older friend from church who lived nearby. She had been very kind to Margaret after her marriage split up. She lifted the phone. 'Joy, could I come round and talk to you? You must have heard about Greg Mitchell.'

31

CHECKPOINTS

- A special school assembly helps children feel a sense of solidarity in which death is acknowledged openly and given a place in the 'system'. The vicar's approach may not be accepted by all teachers but it has a part in the spiritual aspect of death.
- For Foundation level, think of a class activity to try to help the children understand the changes brought about by death. Caterpillars turning into butterflies is a helpful analogy.
- For Year 3, give time and space to encourage children to:
  - try to identify their feelings and express them in an appropriate way, bearing in mind that most children of 7 and 8 need help in recognizing feelings and will probably only get as far as sadness, hurt, fear, and anger
  - clarify their relationship with the child who has died—what bereavement means to them—and express it
  - acknowledge unfinished business, which may be very important to them, and help them to find a way of dealing with it
- For Year 6, deal with the children's new awareness that the everyday world is not always a safe place.
- A visit to the parents is hard to do but is almost always appreciated by bereaved parents. The purpose of going is to show that the school valued the child; that he or she was a significant person to the school; and that the staff care about the family. Take things belonging to the child, but ask the parents whether they want them at this stage. Make the visit short. It opens the way for further contact between parents and school.

Chapter 3

EXPLANATIONS ABOUT HEAVEN
AND ETERNAL LIFE

Many adults who find themselves in the situation of having to tell a child that someone they know has died will add that the person has gone to heaven. Sometimes they say 'to be with Jesus'—whether or not they have any religious beliefs. It gives them something positive to offer and suggests that death is not as final as it may appear.

Yet we may also overlook the child's very real feelings of pain and loss by moving on so quickly, and many adults do feel uncomfortable about what they are saying. They may not be at all sure what they believe about heaven and, worse still, they know that there is said to be 'another place' in the afterlife besides heaven.

So what do we say about the elderly man next door who has just died and who had never, to our knowledge, darkened the doors of any church? He has automatically gone to heaven? We just do not know. Neither do we know what was in the man's mind and heart as he drew close to death. The criminal on the cross beside Jesus turned to him in the last hours of his life and acknowledged that, unlike Jesus, he deserved his punishment, and Jesus replied, 'I promise that today you will be with me in paradise' (Luke 23:43). We have to leave the question of whether or not those who have died have gone to heaven in the hands of Jesus. We may feel more comfortable telling our children that our neighbour has gone to be with Jesus.

Christians accept their teaching from Jesus Christ, and on one level it is simple. By following the Lord's Prayer we learn that heaven is where God is: 'Our Father in heaven…' Heaven is where his will of perfect goodness and love is carried out, rather than our will: 'Your will be done on earth as in heaven…' It is where God's power and glory are known: 'For the kingdom, the power and the glory are yours now and for ever…' And unlike life on earth, life in heaven is everlasting.

On another level, Jesus' teaching is more complex. Jesus talks about 'eternal life', which he defined as a relationship with God and with himself, which begins in this world and continues more fully in heaven. The basis of this relationship is love for God and for Christ, active love of other people in this world, and looking to Jesus to forgive us for our wrongdoings.

Children often ask where heaven is, and tend to pursue the question if we point vaguely into the sky. No one knows where heaven is and presumably Jesus would have told us more about it if we could have understood it from our earthly perspective. But he did tell us not to worry. 'Don't be worried! Have faith in God and have faith in me' (John 14:1).

Only John, the visionary, attempts to describe heaven, in the book of Revelation. It is way beyond most people's comprehension. He describes the heavenly city of Jerusalem: 'The glory of God made the city bright. It was dazzling and crystal clear like a precious jasper stone… And the city did not need the sun or the moon. The glory of God was shining on it, and the Lamb (Jesus) was its light' (Revelation 21:11, 23). 'He (God) will wipe all tears from their eyes, and there will be no more death, suffering, crying, or pain. These things of the past are gone for ever' (Revelation 21:4).

We could tell our children that the Bible describes a beautiful city in heaven, of every colour they could imagine, shining with the light of God. There, Jesus and God are close to the people, and there is no unhappiness at all.

Children who have been bereaved may have their own ideas, however—like Ellie, who knew better than her teacher.

JUNIOR CHURCH (5–6 AND 7–8 YEAR OLDS)

Ellie was in Junior Church as usual. Her aunt took her to the 5–6 year olds' corner and had a quiet word with Helen, her teacher. 'She seems perfectly all right. In fact, she doesn't seem to have taken it in at all.'

When all the children had arrived, Mrs Whitaker, the head of Junior Church, led them in a song and then addressed both classes: 'We're all just heartbroken about what happened to Greg Mitchell this week. I thought my class could think of some prayers asking Jesus to take special care of Greg and his mum and dad.

'Helen's class—could you draw some beautiful pictures of heaven? The Bible says it's like a city of shining colours—blues and golds, greens and purples—with sparkling rivers and special trees. And Jesus talks to everyone and makes them happy and well. Do you think you could do that? We'll put your pictures up on the wall in church for everyone to see.'

❖

The children in Helen's class settled down with their pens and paper —all, that is, except Ellie. She just sat and twisted her hair as well as sucking her thumb.

'What are you going to draw, Ellie?' Helen gave the little girl a clean piece of paper. 'What will you draw first? A lovely river? Jesus and Greg?'

Ellie said nothing. She gave a big sigh, then took a brown pen and drew a bed and a figure lying in it with eyes wide open.

'Is that Greg?' asked Helen.

'He's hurting so he's in hospital. They won't let me see him, but he'll be better for the funeral.'

'What makes you think that, Ellie?'

'Mum said. He's coming back in a big car.'

'Ellie, they will only bring his body back home for a short time before the funeral. He can't come back as Greg. I'm sorry—but he's died.'

'He is coming back.' Ellie's voice rose to a shout. 'You're stupid anyway,' and she pushed the crayons off the table.

❖

Helen winced. She realized that it was all very well talking about heaven to those who were not closely involved, but that was not where Ellie was. Helen felt very concerned about the child's insistence that her brother would come back. She was at a loss as to what to do. Luckily Kate, the teenage helper, moved close to Ellie and said, 'Why don't we play that game when you write a letter down and I have to guess what the word is?'

Ellie smiled. 'Can I sit on your knee? Auntie Jean lets me sleep in her bed.' Helen breathed a sigh of relief as the two settled down happily together side by side. She guessed that Ellie was not getting the comfort she needed at home just now.

Mrs Whitaker glanced at some of the prayers the children had written: 'Jesus, I know you love Greg but it wasn't very nice of you to let him die. Can you make it up to him? Love Michelle.'

'Dear God, I cried last night when I thought of Greg. Could you help his mum and dad because they might cry all night? Amen. Jasmine.'

'Jesus, please look after Greg. He would like to fly very fast. Amen. Alan.'

The vicar did not seem to be as concerned as Helen was when she told him about Ellie's conviction that Greg would come back. 'Ellie's reaction is pretty normal for her age,' he said. 'She can't understand what is going on, and besides, there'll be more going on in her head than she'll tell us. Do you know who she feels safe with, and who she might talk to?'

'She looked very safe with Kate,' said Helen. 'And Kate said she was sleeping with Auntie Jean.'

'Ah, Jean might be the right one,' said Oliver. 'I'll have a word with her when I go round. But really, Helen, you sound as if you handled everything well. It didn't sound easy.'

'I didn't handle Ellie well,' said Helen miserably. 'It was Kate who knew what to do.'

JUNIOR CHURCH (9–11 YEAR OLDS)

Gareth was not in church that morning. His teachers had met together the previous day to look at resources they could possibly use with his class. They decided to look at a play with the children to give a biblical perspective to life after death. They might even do it for the whole church after Easter if the class liked it.

❖

A PLAY: ETERNAL LIFE—NOW AND FOR EVER

SCENE 1

On the shore of the Sea of Galilee, Peter is unloading a basket of fish and nets from his boat, watched at a short distance by a boy aged about eleven.

Boy: Can I help you, sir?

Peter: I'm just about through, thanks. I've got to be off now.

Boy: Where are you going? Can I come with you?

Peter: Come with me? Of course not! I'm off to Jerusalem for the Passover.

Boy: Hey, I'm going to Jerusalem for the Passover. It's my first time. Could I come with you instead of going with my parents?

Peter: Look, lad, you don't even know me. You go home to your parents now.

Boy: Sir, I do know you. You're Simon Peter, aren't you? You were with Jesus that day on the mountain when he was talking to hundreds and hundreds of people.

Peter: You knew Jesus?

Boy: Oh yes. I was with Grandad and Jesus was talking about eternal life. I didn't understand, but Grandad got ever so excited about it. He wanted to talk to Jesus that day but there were too many people around. They had stayed so long listening to Jesus that it was past their dinnertime and past their teatime too. But Mum had given me a packed lunch in case I was out all day, so I gave it to Jesus and, do you know what, he made it enough for everyone... thousands of them! Jesus did a miracle on my lunch!

Peter: Bless my soul! I can see it now. You were the boy with the five barley loaves and the two fishes! (*Puts his hand on the boy's shoulder*) I never even found out your name.

Boy: I'm Reuben. Sir... Peter... please could I meet you again? I want to know if Grandad has eternal life—whatever that is. You see, when we got home after seeing Jesus, he was ill and then he died. But he didn't mind dying. He said Jesus would give him eternal life. But he hasn't, has he?

Peter: I'm sorry about your grandad, Reuben. He knew Jesus well, then?

Reuben: Oh yes. He used to go and listen to Jesus whenever he could. That's why he took me that day.

Peter: Look, I've got to go now, but I've got an idea. When you're in Jerusalem, why don't you come to the house where John and I will be staying? Then we can talk about it some more. And John's your man on the subject of eternal life. I'll write a note to your father now, and give him our address in Jerusalem. All right? (*Writes note*)

Reuben: Thank you, Sir. I can't wait to tell my dad that I've met you and I'm going to meet John in Jerusalem... (*Takes Peter's note and runs off*) Bye. See you.

At Peter's lodgings in Jerusalem. Inside the house, Peter, John and another man are sitting round a table which is set for a meal with bread and wine. There is a knock on the door. Enter Reuben.

Peter:	Reuben, hello! Come and sit down. You'll recognize John, of course…
John:	Hello, Reuben.
Peter:	And this is Paul. We're just getting to know him. He met Jesus after Jesus had died!
Reuben:	Really? Could I meet him again, too?
Peter:	Hang on, Reuben. I'll give thanks now, and then we can talk over the meal.

Peter takes the bread and lifts it up.

Peter:	Blessed are you, Lord God of all creation. In your goodness you have given us this food for our nourishment. Give us the knowledge of your presence and love. Be with us, Lord Jesus, in the breaking of the bread. Amen.

Silence.

Reuben:	*(Looking round)* Is Jesus here? I can't see him.
John:	No, you can't see him. But Jesus taught us to remember him especially when we eat together, and he said he would be with us always through his Spirit. He is here to his friends—those who know him and love him.
Reuben:	But I want to know him too. I thought he was terrific.
John:	You can know him, Reuben. You can talk to him in your prayers and he will make himself known to you. And knowing Jesus in this life is the beginning of eternal life.
Reuben:	What? I don't get it. But you mean I can talk to Jesus whenever I want, now he's in heaven? Just me and him together?

Peter: You and Jesus together. And your grandad will be able to talk to Jesus now—and see him and go round with him all the time.

Reuben: Mmm… but how did Grandad get to heaven? It's a bit hard to get what you mean.

John: I know. We didn't understand at first, did we Peter? But, one day, Jesus made it all clear to us. I remember his words as if it were yesterday. 'Don't be worried!' he said. 'Have faith in God and have faith in me. There are many rooms in my Father's house. I wouldn't tell you this, unless it was true. I am going there to prepare a place for each of you. After I have done this, I will come back and take you with me. Then we will be together. You know the way to where I am going.'[1]

Reuben: That sounds like Jesus all right. You think you understand. But then you're not sure.

John: It means that Jesus had prepared a special home for your grandad in heaven as soon as your grandad started to know him. When your grandad died, Jesus would have taken his spirit to be with him in heaven.

Reuben: How do you mean?

Paul: Right. Let me explain this. Think of a plant, Reuben, like a stalk of wheat, or perhaps a sunflower. It grows very tall in the spring, produces huge yellow flowers in the summer, and then at the end of the summer it dies. OK? Now—can you tell me what's right in the centre of that flower?

Reuben: Big black and grey seeds. I planted one once and it grew into another sunflower.

Paul: Good. Then you know that each seed contains the life inside it to grow into another plant. Now think of your grandad. He had a body that you could see, and he also had a spirit that you couldn't see. His spirit was the part of him that loved Jesus and loved you too, and helped him to make beautiful things. His spirit is what made

Grandad such a wonderful person. When he died, his body was finished, like the sunflower. But his body contained inside it his spirit, which will now grow into a new grandad. God will have given your grandad a new body, a spiritual body which will live for ever.

Reuben: That's why he didn't mind dying. Well, it's all right for him, isn't it? But... I won't ever see him again.

Peter: It is sad for those who are left behind. But you will see him again when you go to heaven. John, could you make it a bit clearer to Reuben how knowing Jesus now is the beginning of eternal life?

John: It was something we heard Jesus say on that last night he was with us... He was talking to God as if he were right there beside him and he said, 'Eternal life is to know you, the only true God, and to know Jesus Christ, the one you sent.'[2]

Reuben: But Grandad *did* know God—he used to pray to him every morning and night—and he knew Jesus, too. Does that mean Grandad had eternal life before he died?

Paul: That's right! And when your grandad died, Jesus would take his spirit to be with him in heaven, and he'd get to know Jesus better, like a close friend. It all starts now— what Jesus called eternal life—and carries on after you die.

Reuben: I think I get what you mean...

John: Jesus will help you to understand. He is making himself known to you already. Go on talking and praying to him, Reuben, and he'll show you all you need to know.

Pause.

John: (*Standing up*) Jesus said, 'God loved the people of this world so much that he gave his only Son, so that everyone who has faith in him will have eternal life and never really die.'[3]

41

All freeze, Peter and Paul leaning forward toward Reuben, and Reuben smiling, with hands slightly uplifted.

1   JOHN 14:1–4
2   JOHN 17:3
3   JOHN 3:16

❖

THE CHURCH SERVICE

Oliver MacKenzie was not looking forward to the service that morning. The death of a child was surely the worst possible scenario to try to explain to the people who would be coming to church that day. The whole community had been shocked by Greg's fatal accident, and he knew that some who did not usually come to church would come today. They would want explanations about how the God he loved so passionately could have let it happen. They would want assurances about life after death. They would want to know how the Christian faith could help in a situation like this. And he would be expected to explain, reassure, help, respond over the most basic issues with which people had struggled ever since the world began.

'Oh, God, why are you such a mystery?' he asked. 'Why don't you protect us from danger and prevent us from having accidents like this?'

As he prepared himself in the vestry, he wondered anew at the heightened sense of spiritual awareness that death brings. 'Be present in the hearts of these people,' he prayed, 'and speak to them of your tender love and purposes for them through this service. Amen.' Then he went out to the front of the church to greet the congregation.

'A very warm welcome to all of you here today. The service will be as usual, but we shall be thinking particularly of the tragedy that has happened this week to Greg Mitchell and I shall try to address some of the questions people are asking. Let us begin by singing hymn number 57…'

JESUS AND LIFE AFTER DEATH

Oliver had decided to change one of the Bible readings prescribed for the day to include one of John's visions of God's heavenly kingdom in the book of Revelation. It describes a great multitude from every nation, who had been made pure through Jesus, worshipping God and living under his protection. Oliver read it himself, concluding, 'They will never hunger or thirst again, and they won't be troubled by the sun or any scorching heat. The Lamb (Jesus) in the centre of the throne will be their shepherd. He will lead them to streams of life-giving water, and God will wipe all tears from their eyes' (Revelation 7:16–17).

He referred back to the passage in his sermon. 'Some of you may like to think of Jesus caring tenderly for Greg now, healing him from the shock of that terrible accident, and any other hurts in his life, cleansing any infections that had crept into his character, bringing out all those lovely parts of his spirit that some of you knew so well—his sense of fun and adventure, his friendly, sharing nature, his enthusiasm for life—and letting him explore the kingdom of heaven.

'As you probably know, all the main religions teach that there is life after death. Jesus' teaching is distinctive, however. He taught that it is he who prepares us for eternal life, and he who stays with us as we come into the presence of God.

'He prepares us as we accept him as the Son of God who has the power to forgive us for our sins—meaning the way we try to live without him. Each day we need to look at ourselves to see if we are living the life of love and grace and truth that he told us to live; and each day we will find that we need to ask his forgiveness for living in our own self-centred way. Then we start again, with his help. When we finally come face to face with God, we come as those who have been made pure by Jesus, and ready to live with him in his heavenly kingdom.

'Now a child like Greg did not have the maturity to know all this. In fact, he did not actually come to Junior Church regularly—he was much too busy playing football on Sunday mornings. But Greg had begun to know Jesus and I believe that is enough. I will always remember him last Easter, standing just there in the front of his class singing 'This little light of mine' as if his life depended on it. Perhaps it did.'

Oliver stopped suddenly and fought back the tears that threatened to overwhelm him. 'I'm sure that Greg had begun to know Jesus. Actually, I think most children do, whether they have been brought to church or not.'

DON'T BLAME GOD; BRING GOD'S LOVE
TO THOSE WHO GRIEVE

He paused and leant over the lectern. 'My friends, never think that God causes tragic accidents. He didn't want Greg to die. I'm sure that God suffers terribly when something like this happens—as he did when he had to watch his own Son die on that cross, for us.

'And God is here for us now, suffering with Greg's family. Losing a child is just about the worst thing that can ever happen to parents. Some of you may know. I know. My little girl died of meningitis. No parent ever gets over it. But with time, God's help and other people's love and support, it is possible to learn to live with it.

'So don't leave the Mitchells on their own. Send them cards or letters about Greg to show how much you care. Call briefly with a cake or something you've baked. Ask if there's anything you can do, like shopping, or ironing, or inviting Ellie and Gareth to play—then do it. Don't hold back because you are not sure if it's the "right" thing to do. The family will appreciate your offer even if they don't take it up at the time. They may not be able to feel God's love for them at the moment, but you can bring something of his love by offering what you can in practical ways.

'Now, to him who is able to keep you from falling and to present you before his glorious presence without fault and with great joy—to the only God our Saviour be glory, majesty, power and authority, through Jesus Christ our Lord, before all ages, now and for evermore! Amen' (Jude 1:25, NIV).

CHECKPOINTS

- Be aware of the adult desire to soften the pain of a bereaved child by saying, 'But he's happy with Jesus in heaven now.' The child needs to acknowledge the pain of losing a loved one. The adult's task is to comfort and listen. In any case, we are not in a position to know the whereabouts of the deceased.
- New Testament teaching emphasizes the need for some relationship with Jesus Christ in this life based on love for him and for God, love for our neighbour, and acceptance of forgiveness by him. This relationship then continues into the next life and is called by Jesus 'eternal life'.
- This New Testament emphasis presents difficulties when talking about someone who is not a professed Christian. We cannot judge the state of another's faith. In the end we have to leave in Jesus' hands the question of whether or not those who have died continue life in heaven.
- Some five-year-olds find it difficult to grasp the finality of death. Furthermore, they may think that they might have caused it or that they can 'magic' people back. A trusted adult needs to hear what the child is saying and, in a comforting environment, reassure and help them to accept the fact that the dead person will not come back.

Here are four New Testament passages which talk about what happens after death:

- 1 Corinthians 15:35–38, 42, 44: Here Paul gives the analogy of a plant which dies but whose seed grows into a new plant. So, as our physical body dies, our spirit continues to a new life with a new spiritual body.
- John 14:1–4: In this passage Jesus tells the disciples to trust him. Through his death and resurrection and ascension into heaven he will prepare a 'place' for us in heaven and take us to be with him.
- Revelation 7:16–17: Those who have been made pure by Jesus will live under his care and protection and suffer no more physical or emotional pain.
- Revelation 21:11, 23: John tells of his vision of the heavenly city, shining with the glory of God.

Chapter 4

EXPLANATIONS ABOUT THE FUNERAL, CREMATION AND THE ROLE OF THE FUNERAL DIRECTOR

Children who have been bereaved suddenly find that their world has changed overnight—for the worse. They themselves are no longer anywhere near the centre of it. Parents are not parenting; the atmosphere in the house is tense, unhappy and often foreboding; meals are not what they were; boundaries are moved, routines dropped, and most of the signs that used to mean stability and security are not there any more.

One way in which we can help our bereaved children is to give them clear explanations about what is happening around them. Another way is to ensure that some of the old familiar structures like school, out-of-school activities and playing with friends are still in place, but with space and time out when necessary.

Explanations will need to include the funeral, the burial or cremation, and where the body is between the death and the funeral. Failure to explain these things can give rise to all sorts of weird and fearful imaginings. Although it is much more usual to include children at funerals and even cremations these days, adults still show a tendency to want to protect the child. Yet if children are told what is going on, and if they are allowed to participate in arrange-ments for the funeral and in the funeral itself, the way is cleared of misunderstandings, and they feel a valued part of their family again and better able to cope with their bereavement.

The general rule, if there is such a thing, is to ask children whether or not they wish to go to the funeral and, if so, to make sure they have the support they will need. And if they do express a wish to see the body, or to go to the burial or cremation, it is wise to let them do so, again with support. Children seem to know instinctively what is right for them, though they may change their minds several times before the event.

Parents are not likely to be able to think clearly about their children's needs at this time. Let us look at how ten-year-old Gareth and five-year-old Ellie are feeling after the death of their brother, listen to the vicar's explanation about what a funeral is for, and hear the story of Ed the undertaker. You may have to take their place in explaining these things and in helping children to feel more secure, more cared for and more involved.

THE FUNERAL

'I wish someone had explained it all to me.'

Gareth asked his friend Mike if he would come to the funeral with him. Mike had invited Gareth round to his house on the Saturday after the accident and they had enjoyed playing together. It was like it used to be before Greg had died. Gareth had felt free to laugh and shout and play again; it had even felt good to be told off by Mike's mum for throwing their coats on the floor.

Mike was the only one who seemed to understand how awful it all was. His father had died only last year. When Gareth asked for a second helping of toad-in-the-hole, Mike had commented, 'I don't suppose your mum is cooking much, is she?' And when they were pushing their bikes up the hill, Mike said, 'My mum has only just begun to be my mum again. She lost it somehow when Dad died.'

'I think my mum has lost it,' said Gareth. 'Dad too. He's kind of not there. Not even there for Mum. She talks to me instead of Dad. It's weird.'

'No one ever asked me what I wanted,' said Mike. 'Everyone talked to Mum and didn't take any notice of me.'

'That's just it,' said Gareth. They walked on in silence. Then Gareth said, 'I can't seem to get it right with Mum. She asked me what kind of flowers I thought Greg would like on his coffin, and when I said I didn't think Greg would like any flowers but why not have oranges and bananas and leaves and conkers, she started to cry and said I was too young to understand. One minute she treats me like a grown-up and the next minute like a child. It's weird.'

❖

They reached the top of the hill and paused for a while. Then Gareth said, 'Mike, you wouldn't come to the funeral with me, would you?'

'Um… don't know. My dad's funeral was a bit much. I didn't know what was going on most of the time. I just sat there on my own while my older brother put his arm round my mum.'

Gareth thought about it. 'I guess Dad will do that—and Auntie Jean will be there for Ellie if she goes. I don't want to sit on my own. The vicar asked if I'd go round to church on Monday so he could explain what will happen. Ellie won't come. I don't really want to go.'

'I'll come,' said Mike suddenly. 'I wish someone had explained it all to me. Come on, Gareth. Let's go!'

For the next few minutes, Gareth forgot all about Greg in the exhilaration of whizzing downhill on his bike with the cool wind blowing in his face.

SHOULD CHILDREN GO TO THE FUNERAL?

Abby, Greg's friend, and her mum were there when Gareth and Mike arrived at the church. The vicar, Oliver, had mentioned to the head-teacher that he would meet any children who wanted to go to the funeral after school on Monday, to prepare them for it. Margaret had phoned round a few parents of the children she thought might want to go. Abby's mother had been one of them and that evening Oliver had received a very angry phone call from her. 'I'd just like to let you know that I don't think it's right for children as young as seven to go to funerals. Abby has gone on and on about wanting to go and I'm certainly not going to allow it. I don't think you should encourage it either.'

Oliver loathed angry phone calls—especially in the middle of tea. He tried not to respond to the criticism. 'Why does Abby want to go to the funeral, Mrs Read?'

'I don't know. I can't get any sense out of her. She just keeps saying that Greg was her friend and gets very upset. I can't do anything with her.'

'Mrs Read, children do go to funerals these days, if they really want to. It seems to help them cope. What's more, they can regret it for the rest of their lives if they're not allowed to go. Abby is grieving for Greg.'

'Well, I can't take time off work to bring her, so that's the end of it.'

Oliver pressed on. 'Gareth's friend Mike is coming. He seems keen to know what the funeral is all about, as no one explained anything at his father's funeral.'

'Oh, is Angela letting Mike go? Well… I might think about it…'

WHAT IS A FUNERAL FOR?

Oliver had taken some orange juice and a bag of sweets for the three children. He and Abby's mum sat in the children's corner with Gareth, Mike and Abby and chatted generally. Then Oliver asked, 'Does anyone know why we have a funeral for someone who has died?'

No one said anything, so Oliver went on. 'It's when everyone there—Greg's family and his friends—say goodbye to Greg. Good-byes are important, and we didn't have time to say goodbye to Greg.'

'No, he just went away, and we were going to make a secret den and he was coming to my birthday party,' said Abby.

Gareth nodded. 'It leaves me feeling sort of left behind.'

'I know,' said Oliver. 'We don't want to say goodbye but since he has gone away, as Abby says, it would make us feel better if we did.'

'I gave my dad the swimming certificate I'd got the day he died,' said Mike. 'I put it under the flowers on the coffin. I wanted to give him something, and he would have been so proud of me.'

'Some people do give something like that,' said Oliver. 'It's their way of saying goodbye.'

❖

'Another thing we do at funerals is to think together about the person who has died. I'll be talking about Greg. I'll try to paint as true a picture as I can from what his parents and teachers have told me. And Gareth, I'd like you to think of anything about Greg that you would like me to say.'

Gareth laughed unexpectedly. 'I remember the time he took away Dr Brown's chair just as he was about to sit down. You should have seen him! By the time he'd got his balance, Greg had done a runner. Greg played a lot of funny tricks on people. Would you say that in your talk?'

'I'll mention his tricks,' Oliver promised, 'but I won't tell that story because Dr Brown might be there. There will be a lot of people at the funeral.'

'I've written a poem about Greg,' said Abby. She fished it out of her pocket and showed it to Oliver. 'I could read it, if you like.'

'That's beautiful, Abby,' said Oliver, 'but it could be hard for you to read it aloud at the funeral if you were upset.'

'I could read it,' said Mike. 'I wouldn't cry.'

'I'll see what Greg's parents feel about that,' said Oliver. 'It sounds a good idea.'

❖

'The next important part of a funeral is to give Greg back to God.'

'I'm going to ask Jesus to give him a big hug,' said Abby. 'Greg likes hugs.'

'That's just what Jesus will want to do,' said Oliver. 'Greg will be all right with Jesus. You know that, don't you?'

'Yes, I know that,' said Gareth. 'But I just wish he was still here.' He put his head in his hands. 'I'm sorry. I can't help crying. I don't know how I'll live without my kid brother.' Abby's mum hugged Gareth to her and Oliver felt his own tears coming. 'It's all right to cry, Gareth. Grown-up men like me cry when something like this happens.'

❖

Oliver handed round the sweets, then went over what would happen on Thursday from the arrival of Greg's body in the big black car to the moment when he would put his hand on the coffin and say the words of commendation into the hands of God.

He paused for a moment and Gareth said, 'What happens next?'

Abby's mum got up. 'We've got to go now. I think I'll be able to take Thursday off work to bring Abby to the funeral. Goodbye, Gareth. Bye, Mike.'

THE CREMATION

Oliver looked a bit surprised. 'I'm sorry they didn't stay to talk about what happens next. It's important to face the next part. For after we've commended Greg's spirit to God, we then commit his body to be cremated.'

'You mean he's burned,' said Gareth bluntly.

'I mean it's burned,' said Oliver firmly. 'Greg isn't in his body any more and it needs to be buried or cremated.'

'Are you quite, quite sure that he won't feel anything?' asked Gareth.

'Absolutely sure, because there's no life in the body now,' said Oliver. 'It will start to decay if it's just left.'

'Like our cat that was run over,' said Mike. 'We couldn't just leave him by the side of the road. There were flies all over his face.'

'The cremation is done very properly,' said Oliver hastily. 'After the funeral service in the church, Greg's body will be taken in the big black car to a place called the crematorium, which is like a little church. I shall then commit his body to be cremated and say some prayers. Then, either curtains are drawn round the coffin, or we can just leave it there and walk out. The coffin goes into a special oven place where it is burned and the ashes are given back to the family to be buried, or scattered in a favourite place.'

'My dad's ashes are over there'—Mike pointed to the graveyard— 'and his name is on a big stone. Mum goes there sometimes and takes flowers. I went on my birthday—it didn't seem right to have a birthday without Dad—and I talked to him, though I know he isn't really there.'

'Ellie wants to see Greg,' said Gareth suddenly. 'I mean his body —but I don't think I want to. I think dead bodies are scary.'

'They are not really scary, you know,' said Oliver, 'Why don't you meet my friend, Ed, who takes care of bodies from the time of death until the time of the funeral. Funnily enough, he loves his job and feels it is very important.'

'Would he come here?' asked Gareth. 'I wouldn't like to meet any dead bodies at his place.'

'Don't worry,' said Oliver. 'If it's all right with your mum and dad, I'll invite him round to the vicarage. OK?'

'Hey, can I come too?' asked Mike.

ED THE UNDERTAKER'S STORY

Ed was an undertaker. His proper title was 'funeral director' but Ed preferred the term 'undertaker'. His father had been an undertaker and his grandfather before him. 'Always treat the dead with respect,' his father used to say. 'You don't know who they have been or what they have done in their lives. And be kind to their relatives. Dying is a sad business for those left behind.' So Ed was always nice to his customers. He wanted to do as good a job for them as his father had done—and his grandfather before him.

Ed was at the vicarage before the boys arrived and stood up to greet them. 'Which is Gareth? Pleased to meet you, Gareth. Tragic about your brother. I'll look after him with great care until the day of the funeral.'

Gareth was surprised and pleased at Ed's remark. No one had said anything like that to him since the accident.

'It's a bit scary,' he said. 'My brother Greg—dead... like... a dead body.'

'It is the saddest thing that could have ever happened,' said Ed. 'And it's my job to help people not to be nervous of seeing the body and not to be all worried and anxious about the funeral. I arrange everything.'

❖

Ed told them all about his job, beginning from the time he took the body from the house or hospital and brought it to his funeral home.

'My first job is to give the bodies a good wash and freshen up,' he said, 'and to make them look as nice as possible for the family to come and see them. I dress them in the clothes that their family want them in. And while I'm doing that, the lads in the workshop make a specially made-to-measure coffin and line the inside with white satin material or whatever colour the family want.'

'Doesn't it feel sort of funny, to put clothes on a dead body?' asked Mike.

'Not at all,' replied Ed. 'I've been brought up to it. I used to watch my father when I was just a young lad, and then help him when I was older. He used to talk to them sometimes. "It's all right now, Gran," he would say. "No more painful joints." He used to get upset when it was a child, though,' he added, 'and so do I.'

There was a silence. Ed sighed and continued, 'Anyway, when the day of the funeral comes, we clean and polish the cars—first the hearse, which is the one that carries the coffin, and then the others to take the relatives or friends in.'

❖

'What kind of cars are they?' asked Gareth.

'Daimlers,' said Ed with pride. 'Big, black, shiny Daimlers.'

'Will I go in a Daimler?' Gareth's face lit up. 'I could wave to people out of the window.'

'Oh yes. Only the best cars for this job,' said Ed. 'And our best clothes—black suit, white shirt and black tie. Sometimes we even wear top hats. Just before the time of the funeral, we carry the coffin out to the hearse and arrange the flowers that the family have brought on the top, so that it looks as beautiful as possible.

'Then we set off in convoy to the house where the person used to live, pick up the relatives and drive to the church or the crematorium—wherever the funeral is to take place.'

'Do you like driving the car?' asked Gareth.

'I love it,' said Ed simply. 'It goes as smoothly as a bird, even in low gear. I drive very slowly because I'm carrying something very special. All the other cars on the road slow down and give way— as is very right and proper. We stop outside the church or the crematorium and bring the coffin out of the back of the car very carefully.'

❖

'Now comes the tricky part,' said Ed, looking important, 'and it has to be done properly and with dignity. We have to stand at each side of the coffin and lift it very carefully and very smoothly, up and on to our shoulders. When we've got it perfectly balanced, we put our hands down by our sides and walk slowly, in step with each other, into the church behind the vicar. The family usually follow, and when we get to the front of the church we lower the coffin very gently and smoothly on to a stand. The family then take their place at the front of the church and the funeral service begins.

'When the vicar talks about the person who's died, I'm always glad that I've looked after their body with such care. "They've all been important in their own way," my father used to say, "and it's only right that we should commend them into the hands of the Almighty. He knows them better than anyone."'

'How do you get to where it's burnt?' said Gareth.

Ed was not to be hurried. 'The committal of the body to the earth, or cremation, comes after the church part is over. "Dust to dust, ashes to ashes," as they say.

'We now take the body on its last journey to the crematorium or grave.'

'Do we all get in the car again?' Gareth had to know. It was what was keeping him going.

'Yes. I drive the hearse in front and usually only a few members of the family follow in the car behind. The vicar says some prayers, then the words of the committal and then the curtains close.

'I have to say that I don't like that part—the body I've cared for, and the coffin made specially, going to be burnt just like that. But I know it was only the shell of the person who had died.

'If it's a burial, me and the lads have another tricky thing to do. We all gather round the grave…'

'Which is a long deep hole in the ground with mounds of earth piled up,' interrupted Mike. 'I've seen it on TV. Then the coffin goes slowly down into the hole and everyone throws soil over it.'

'And how do you think that coffin gets into the grave?' asked Ed, slightly annoyed. He wanted to be the one to tell the story. 'It's a work of art, I can tell you, getting the straps round the coffin in the right place and lowering it slowly, with dignity, to the bottom of the grave.

'It's a sad job, but as my father always said, "It's your task, son, to make it as smooth as you can for everyone concerned. It's one of the most worthwhile jobs there is."'

At that point, Oliver's wife came in with tea and Coke for the boys. Gareth felt better on the whole. 'Can I still ride home in the Daimler if I don't go to the crematorium?'

ELLIE AND THE FUNERAL HOME

If Gareth was trying hard to be what he thought his parents wanted him to be, Ellie was doing just the opposite. In fact, she seemed to have turned overnight from a sunny-natured, affectionate little girl into a child who angrily demanded the very thing her parents could not give her—the happy family life and normal routine she had always known, with lots of nice Ellie-attention from everyone. When Sue's sister Jean, who was coming in each day to help, offered to take Ellie home with her to sleep, everyone accepted gratefully.

Two nights before the funeral, Ellie crept into Jean's bed in the middle of the night, her own being wet, and said miserably, 'I want to play with Greg; I want him home again with me.' For the umpteenth time, Jean told Ellie that Greg could not come home and, instead of throwing the usual temper tantrum, Ellie said, 'I'll never be mad with Greg again, and I'll give him all my sweet money.' She started to sob loudly and Jean held her close and stroked her hair until the sobs subsided to shudders.

In the morning, when they were getting dressed, Ellie said suddenly, 'I want to see Greg. I need to talk to him, and Mum won't let me. I know where he is. He's in that house at the end of the hospital road with flowers in the window. Can we go now?'

'I'll see what I can do,' promised Jean and while Ellie was finishing breakfast she phoned the vicar. 'Do you think it would be all right for Ellie to see Greg's body if I can persuade Sue to let her?' She told Oliver how difficult Ellie was being, and how she had asked to go. Oliver remembered guiltily that he had promised to get in touch with Jean anyway. 'More children are going to see the body these days. It seems to be what some of them need.' He added, 'He looks all right. Ed has done a good job.'

To Jean's relief, Ellie's parents agreed to let Ellie go with them, as long as Jean was there to take her away and leave them to have some time on their own. Ellie tiptoed over to the open coffin and looked inside. Greg looked as if he were asleep. He wore a red football shirt.

'Greg, I didn't mean it. I was mad because you wouldn't play with me. I didn't mean to say I hated you, really. I cried when you just went off on your roller-blades. I'm sorry it was me who made you go into that car. You can have all my sweet money,' and she put two ten-pence pieces on Greg's chest. 'Bye, Greg,' she whispered, and gently touched Greg's cheek. Ellie's father came over to her.

'Ellie, it wasn't you who made Greg go into that car. It just happened.'

'Nothing you said or thought could have caused Greg's death,' said Sue, 'just as nothing anyone can do will bring him back. Oh Ellie, why didn't you tell us?'

Ellie started crying then, and the three of them hugged each other and wept together.

Jean left them to it. Ellie was in the right place—with her parents, sharing in their grief.

CHECKPOINTS

• The world around children changes suddenly when there is a family bereavement. Their needs may not be able to be met by parents. Children need answers and clear explanations from a trusted adult about what is happening—for example:
  - About the body: they need to know that the body is now 'it', with no feeling, awareness or life in it.
  - About the funeral: what will happen at the funeral? What will happen at the cremation or burial?

• Assume that most school-age children will go to the funeral unless they say they do not want to. Give them the opportunity to see the body, if appropriate and if they ask, and to go to the cremation or grave if they want to. They need to say goodbye in their own way.

- It is worth emphasizing to a four- to six-year-old the actual cause of the death, adding that no one could have caused it by voicing or thinking bad thoughts about the one who has died. It is not uncommon for five-year-olds to fear that they have caused the death in some way.

Chapter 5

RETURNING TO SCHOOL AFTER
A DEATH IN THE FAMILY

Children, like adults, react to the death of someone close to them in their own individual ways. It is difficult for adults who are caring for children in a class or group situation to listen or respond to an individual child for as long as the child needs, as well as coping with the rest of the class. This is why school assistants and helpers in all groups can be invaluable at a time of bereavement. They can make themselves available to go to the children at times of need and take them out of the class, giving them time and space to talk or have a story or simply play. Children may not be able to articulate what is on their minds, but the individual attention gives them the opportunity to try to express themselves in whatever way they can. There is much to be said for 'holding' children where they are, rather than letting them feel alone with themselves and with their thoughts and fears.

Older children of about ten will usually want to appear normal among their peer group and may not seem outwardly affected by the death. Besides, they may be relieved to join in normal activities and to laugh and play with others of their own age for a while. It reassures them that life in the world outside the home is going on as usual. But, like younger children, they may not be able to sustain 'normal life' for long at a time and it has been found helpful for schools to have a 'quiet room' within the school setting to which they can retreat when they cannot cope with classroom activities along with everyone else. Obviously they will need someone to go with them while they catch up on work they have missed, or read books about other children who have been bereaved, or do something creative, or just talk about what is on their mind, if they want to.

Ideally, children need a balance between being appropriately included in family grief and preparations for the funeral and joining in normal life outside the family. It is a balance which is unlikely to be achieved at all times, but we can at least try to ensure that trusted young people or adults are there to offer a reassuring presence.

Children who do not have some of their needs met or acknowledged are likely to carry them into adult life. Past bereavements, and the emotions felt then, have a way of surfacing when triggered off by a later death, and experiences will affect their outlook and their way of dealing with themselves and others. Good counselling can bring to the surface unresolved grief of the past and help to clear the way for a healthier approach to bereavement in general.

GREG'S FIVE-YEAR-OLD SISTER, ELLIE

Ellie returned to school two days after Greg's death. Her teacher, Lorraine, had tried to prepare the class for a sad little Ellie who would need kindness and comfort. Neither Lorraine nor the other children were prepared for the Ellie who bounced into the playground before school and said excitedly, 'My brother's bedroom is empty now because he's dead.'

'It's good to have you back with us, Ellie,' said Lorraine as soon as they were in the classroom. 'Isn't it, children?'

'Yes.' All eyes were on Ellie. What would she say next?

'My Auntie Jean makes me sandwiches with all the crusts cut off. I don't have to have what Greg wants all the time.'

'Auntie Jean sounds very kind,' said Lorraine. It did not look as if Ellie would integrate back into the class until there had been some exchanges between her and the other children. Literacy hour would have to be postponed—yet again. 'I think we should have a special news time together, so that we can tell Ellie what we've been doing and she can tell us about what she's been doing. Ellie, would you like to start?'

Ellie was pleased to be first. 'Well, I'm sleeping at Auntie Jean's and Greg's in a special box at the hospital… I think… He wouldn't play with me before he was dead. Auntie Jean's got a puppy with a white spot on his face.'

'Thank you, Ellie,' said Lorraine. 'We've all been talking about what happens when people die and we've been feeling very sad that Greg won't be at school with us any more. What other news has anyone got?'

'My sister cried at bedtime,' said one child. 'I think she cried all night because she didn't want Greg to be dead. She…'

Ellie interrupted. 'I didn't cry. He's only dead… now… for a day… and a night…'

Lorraine was not sure what Ellie meant. 'We've been thinking about that, too,' she said. 'How Greg is dead in one way but alive in another kind of way.'

'I need the toilet,' said Ellie. 'I can't go on my own.'

Pam, the classroom assistant, went out with her and Ellie took her time, sitting there and singing to herself. By the time they were back, the rest of the class were busy copying letters and words. Ellie's book had been set out for her, and she sat down next to Hollie, sucked her thumb and watched Hollie painstakingly copying the letter 'g' into her literacy book.

Just as she was finishing, Ellie nudged her so sharply that Hollie's pencil made a scribble over the 'g'. Hollie was furious and elbowed Ellie as hard as she could, whereupon Ellie giggled loudly and pushed Hollie off her chair. Pam helped Hollie up and suggested to Ellie that they go over to the comfy corner and have a story.

❖

The day wore on, with Ellie picking fights, demanding all Pam's attention and not settling to anything. Lorraine tried to think of ways of calming her down and suddenly remembered 'Circle Time'. She had been under such pressure lately, these special times had gradually been pushed aside, but now, she felt, might be the right time to reintroduce them.

The children were still familiar with the structure of 'Circle Time' and gathered themselves quietly on the carpet. Lorraine sat on the floor with them as part of the circle, and Pam joined them too, next to Ellie. Lorraine reminded the children of the 'Circle Time' rules.

'Only one person to speak at a time; listen to each other; stay very quiet.

'Can everyone see this shell, all curly and pink and shiny on the inside? We're going to pass it round, and when it's your turn to hold it I want you to curl your hands around it, close your eyes, and say something that makes you feel all nice and peaceful inside. Right?

'I'll start... I feel nice and peaceful when I think of the sea with little waves splashing on the sand. Close your eyes and think of that sea.' She paused for a minute before passing the shell to Hollie.

'I feel nice and peaceful when Dad's in the middle of a story at bedtime.'

The children stayed quiet with their eyes shut. Hollie passed the shell to Ellie and Lorraine held her breath. Ellie's eyes closed as she held the shell and said, 'I feel nice and peaceful when I'm swinging up and down and up and down.' She held on to the shell for a moment, then passed it on and closed her eyes again.

Lorraine felt mightily relieved. When everyone had held the shell, she asked them to get up very quietly and get ready for going home.

❖

Lorraine made a coffee for herself in the staff room and wished it were a gin. Margaret was there with the counsellor. She turned to Lorraine. 'You look drained. Would you like to talk to Adele?'

'I'm all right, thanks. It's just that Ellie was so disruptive, and if it hadn't been for Pam I couldn't have coped.'

'You'd have coped like we used to, with firm discipline,' said Frances, the teacher of Year 4. 'If Ellie had disrupted my class she would have been sent on her own into the corner. It sounds as if she really needed a good smack—but you can't do that nowadays, more's the pity.'

'A smack?' Lorraine felt a surge of anger rising up within her. 'But you don't know what was going on in that child's head. She's so confused and is trying to be all right.'

'That's nothing to do with it,' said Frances. 'If she's disturbing the rest of the class, she needs to be stopped. How else are you going to get through your work?'

Lorraine bit her lip, thinking how very little formal work she had got through that day. Adele came forward. 'How did you cope with Ellie, Lorraine? Did anything seem to help her at all?'

Lorraine told her about 'Circle Time', and how it had finally calmed Ellie at the end of the day. She felt better when Adele commented, 'You do seem to have contained her within the classroom very constructively. You must be exhausted.'

GREG'S TEN-YEAR-OLD BROTHER, GARETH

Gareth did not return to school until just before the funeral. He wanted to—badly—but his mother said she needed him at home. He found that he was a sort of go-between for his parents, who were finding it hard to agree about anything. His dad's voice would get an edge to it and his mum would begin to choke over her words and then break down in tears. 'What do you think, Gareth?' she would say.

Gareth did not know what he thought any more. The worst time so far had been when his mum wanted to talk about what clothes to put on Greg. A shirt and school tie, T-shirt and jeans, or sports wear? His father could not cope with this conversation and went out of the room.

'What do you think, Gareth?'

'I don't know, Mum.'

Gareth felt sick but did not like to go out of the room. In the end he had to go with his mum to a sports shop and watch her ask the assistant about the latest Liverpool club football shirt. 'Do you have one to fit a seven-year-old?'

Gareth willed the assistant not to ask any questions about the seven-year-old. He could not help wishing that he could have a Man United strip. Then he felt awful. That was the funny thing. He felt too awful most of the time even to cry.

When he did go back to school, he felt not quite with it, as if he were living in two worlds but not belonging fully to either. He was glad to see Mike grinning at him from the other side of the class-room, but everything seemed different. He had fallen behind the others in his work and could not join in as he usually did. 'I'll give you some extra homework so you can catch up,' promised Alan.

Out in the playground, he joined in the football but fell and hurt himself. Everyone went on playing as Gareth sat and nursed his leg. He suddenly felt like crying, and kept swallowing as he went back into the classroom. His throat felt sore and swollen. He did not feel at all interested in copying up the science experiments the others had done the day before, but he started to write, gripping his pen so tightly and pressing down so hard that it suddenly snapped. He looked up and saw that two of the others were laughing at him. He tried to laugh too, but felt angry that school as well as home was so awful.

WHEN THE NORMAL SCHOOL SYSTEM IS NOT ENOUGH

As Gareth went with the others for dinner, he felt suddenly overwhelmed by the noise and he panicked. He could not go in. Muttering about forgetting something, he ran back to the classroom, passing a door in the corridor which, unusually, was open. He ran out into the warm sunshine, squeezed through the hedge, and just ran and ran, feeling gloriously free and full of energy again.

He made for the pond where he and Greg used to try to catch fish with their hands, and flung himself down on the warm grass. He felt strangely 'right' within himself and, closing his eyes, he felt that Greg was probably all right. 'Catch any fish up there, Greggy?' He could have sworn he heard a laugh, the chuckling sort of laugh that was Greg's when he laughed with you.

Gareth sat up and threw stones into the water. It seemed as if Greg were with him. He walked on to the wood where he had once built a tree-house with Greg. Part of it was still there. He leaned against the tree trunk and let the tears flow and the sobs well up from the pit of his stomach.

After dinner, Alan went out into the playground to check that Gareth was all right. He was feeling bad, as he had not done anything about setting up somewhere quiet for Gareth to retreat to. When he could not see him, he went to the classroom and waited as everyone came in—everyone but Gareth. 'Anyone seen Gareth?' he asked. When the children thought about it, no one remembered seeing him at dinner.

Alan told them to get on with an exercise and went to see Margaret in the headteacher's office. 'Gareth's disappeared. No one has seen him since before lunch. He seemed all right this morning.'

Alarm bells began to ring for Margaret as she and the school secretary searched every room in the school and every corner of the playground. She knew that the next step was to phone Gareth's parents to see if he was at home. Gareth's father answered the phone. Gareth was not there.

'Do you think we should inform the police?' asked Margaret, with difficulty. Gareth's father sighed. 'Can we leave it a bit longer? I just couldn't tell Sue at the moment. I'll go out and look for him round here.' They both said they would ring each other if Gareth turned up.

Margaret put the phone down. How could she have let it happen?

The staff room was quiet at the end of the afternoon. The police had been in and out and no one wanted to go home until there had been some news of Gareth. Margaret could hear Frances' voice going on and on to Adele. 'It's because of the lack of discipline in this place. No child would have dared leave the school when Mrs Scott was here.'

Adele tried to make some kind of answer. 'You know, Gareth probably just needed to have a bit of space on his own for a while. He'll probably turn up at home before long.'

'But that's not the point,' said Frances. 'He shouldn't have been allowed...'

'Frances—shut up and get out. Now.' The loud voice came from Margaret. Frances looked stunned, picked up her bag and left the room. Margaret, shocked herself by her own rudeness, also left—by the other door.

As soon as they had gone, the staff began to talk about them. It was a good distraction.

FRANCES: A BEREAVEMENT OF THE PAST

Frances drove home furious with Margaret for shouting at her like that in front of all the other teachers. 'Shut up and get out!' The words seemed to strike a chord in her somewhere.

'Frances, shut up and get out. Now...' It was her father's voice speaking to the ten-year-old Frances as she shook her dying mother and cried, 'Mummy, don't go. Don't leave me.' Her mother tried to speak but no words came, and she gave a great sigh and closed her eyes. Frances screamed and her father grabbed hold of her. 'Shut up and get out...'

Frances never knew whether her mother had died at that point, or whether her father had had a few quiet moments with her before she died. She broke out into a cold sweat now as she realized how she had spoiled what could have been a peaceful death, not only for her father but for her mother too. She had not thought of it like that before. At the time, she had been so angry that she had not been told how ill her mother was, though everyone else, including her older sister, seemed to know. And when she came in from school one day in the following week and found her uncle and aunts and other relatives in the house, and realized that her mother's funeral had taken place that afternoon—without her—she was utterly devastated.

Frances had never felt completely part of the family after that. Her form teacher had been very kind to her, she remembered, and praised her work. She began to focus on school and work and got excellent reports and even the prize for the best pupil in her year. Her father had been pleased with these reports. He was relieved that his younger daughter seemed to have got over her mother's death so easily...

A figure flew past the windscreen and Frances slammed on the brakes. A boy was picking himself up from the pavement—a boy she knew. 'Gareth! Oh, thank goodness you're here.'

Gareth looked frightened. 'I had to get away. Don't make me go back to school—or home. I'm all right.' As Gareth made to go away, Frances took him gently into her car. 'Sit here and have a drink of water from this bottle while I phone school on my mobile.'

She got through to the school secretary, and asked her to inform the police that she had found Gareth and would take him home. The police could ring her later. She put the phone down and turned to Gareth.

'We've all been worried about you. But they know you're safe now. Would you mind if I walked back with you instead of going in the car? We can take our time. Where did you go, anyway?'

Frances felt a strong sense of identity with Gareth. As they walked along, he told her how awful the morning had been and how awful it was at home. Frances just listened sympathetically, which was unusual for her. When they came within sight of Gareth's road, he said, 'I'll be all right now—and I will go home. Bye.'

As Frances watched him run off home, she began to compare her own experience of bereavement with that of Gareth, at the same age. But when she thought about the actual death of her mother, she had to shut off, as she always had done right up until that afternoon.

She also managed to shut her mind off from Margaret by preparing lessons for the rest of the evening, but in the early, dark hours of the next morning, both Margaret's words and those of her father all came back. She took sleeping tablets to shut it all out again.

❖

Frances woke with one of her dreaded migraines and knew that she could not go to school. She dialled the school number with difficulty, and spent the morning just trying to survive the pain in her head. She felt as if there were a screaming from somewhere deep inside her... like the screaming of a child...

She had to find some way of stopping herself thinking about that awful scene at her mother's deathbed. By afternoon the pain in her head was subsiding with the help of tablets, but the screaming sensation was louder. She made the decision to phone the doctor and was given an appointment that evening.

'I need something to help me cope with the stress situation at school,' she told him. 'Can you prescribe something that will calm me down?'

She went over some of the scene in the staff room and the effect it had had on her last night.

'Would you consider seeing a counsellor?' said Dr Brown. 'Medication is not going to solve your problem.'

Frances was disappointed. 'Well, if you won't help I suppose I could try the counsellor at school.' She sighed. What did counsellors do, anyway?

A COUNSELLING SESSION ABOUT A BEREAVEMENT OF THE PAST

'It's good of you to fit me in,' she began as she sat down in Adele's counselling room. 'What I need is a few techniques for coping with stress. You're qualified to do that, aren't you?'

Adele felt horrified to see Frances after the scene in the staff room. 'Stress counselling isn't just about giving techniques. We'd need to explore the nature of the stress. We'd need to look at why you are reacting as you do, and then consider ways you might feel you could deal with it.'

'That sounds a very long way round,' said Frances. 'I'll try to explain it more clearly. You know the situation at school and you saw the way the Head lost her temper. I just need to be able to cope with the stress caused by other people.'

There was a long silence. Then Adele said very gently, 'Counselling is about you, Frances. I can only help you look at yourself and why you feel as you do. Your stress is different from anyone else's. We would need to talk about you.'

❖

The interview was not going the way Frances had planned. She was about to get up but the pain of her mother's death swept over her again. 'Would it help in controlling my thoughts?' she asked. 'That's what I really need.'

'It could help you bear your own thoughts by bringing them up to the surface in a safe place and looking at them rationally. It could help you come to terms with them so that you don't need to be in conflict with them any more.'

Frances yielded an inch. 'I don't see how, but anyway, if I did talk about myself how do I know that you wouldn't tell anyone else—like Margaret?'

'Counselling is completely confidential—unless I felt that you were going to harm yourself or anyone else. The only person I would need to talk to is my supervisor, but that is completely confidential too and your name need never even be mentioned. Counselling is very professional, you know.'

'Well, I could start, and see if it works…'

❖

It was not until the next session that Frances mentioned what was really troubling her. She started with the row with Margaret. 'I can't

forget it. She lost her temper and spoke to me as if I were a child…'
She stopped as the tears came into her eyes.

'What upset you particularly about the way Margaret spoke to you?' asked Adele gently. There was a long silence. Eventually Frances began to talk about how it had brought back her father's words at that awful scene when her mother was dying.

'Do you think you could go over that scene—but as the little girl Frances? What did you think as you went into that room and saw your mother looking so ill?'

As she talked about it for the first time, Frances relived the unbearable realization that her mother was going to die. Clutching her head in her hands, she rocked to and fro as she felt again the shock of not being included—the rejection, the belittlement. Adele put her hand over Frances' and let her cry and cry.

'And you've buried all those unbearable feelings for all those years,' she commented.

'I'm going to make us a cup of tea. The adult Frances needs it.' A few minutes later, when Frances was feeling calmer, Adele asked, 'Can you forgive the little ten-year-old Frances now?'

'I didn't know any better, did I? I'm not sure that I can forgive my father, though.'

'You might in time. Be kind to yourself just now.'

CHECKPOINTS

- Give time to young children who are bereaved, to talk about what is happening in their lives. Be aware that older children might be carrying more responsibility than they feel able to and may need space and permission to 'be where they are'.

- When planning activities for a school class or other group, try to have assistants or helpers who can offer individual attention to troubled children, or go with them away from the group if necessary. These children may be able to integrate with others in a group situation for short times only.

- If possible, have another room, or corner of a large room, with books and playthings and soft toys, as a quiet place of retreat for children who are upset.
- Be aware of past bereavements in adults' lives, affecting their present attitudes toward bereavement. Counselling can help, but only if it is really wanted.
- Some teachers are resistant to the idea of counselling because they are used to keeping themselves together and coping with classes however bad they are feeling. The counselling process may need to be explained to them.

Chapter 6

TRAINING DAY ON THE REACTIONS AND NEEDS OF PRIMARY SCHOOL CHILDREN WHO HAVE BEEN BEREAVED

The non-statutory guidelines for Personal, Social and Health Education, and Citizenship, introduced alongside the National Curriculum in August 2000, acknowledge the area of feelings as something that needs to be addressed—for Key Stage 1, at any rate. They recommend that pupils at this key stage 'should be taught to recognize, name and deal with their feelings in a positive way'. If only these guidelines were recommended and followed throughout the various key stages into adulthood, the world would be filled with well-balanced, open-minded people, well able to face life and death in a reasonably straightforward and constructive way.

All theories about the process of bereavement grief bring out the emotional states of numbness, anger, guilt, yearning, anxiety and helplessness, in adults and in children. These emotions can be intensely painful if the relationship with the one who has died was close. Some adults may be able to recognize and name these feelings on their own; others need help. Children, however, may struggle with what seems like a mass of unidentifiable hurts that simmer inside them and erupt from time to time in a way that no one around seems to understand.

The special emotional needs of children who have been bereaved are now being acknowledged in educational circles, and there are courses provided for those who want to be able to respond more sensitively and effectively. There is also talk of introducing 'death education' into schools. If a child in the class does experience the death of someone close to them, the teacher may wish to take the opportunity to educate the class and answer questions about death constructively, as well as introducing awareness to the other children about how the bereaved child might feel. Other adults in the children's lives may well avoid the subject.

This chapter gives a flavour of what could be included in a training course, covering both facts and feelings, although it cannot offer the participative or experiential aspect which is a must for the personal understanding of bereavement. Nor can it offer depth or detail. But do come as an observer to this training day on 'The reactions and needs of primary school children who are bereaved'.

FEELING THE NEED FOR TRAINING

As headteacher of a school that had experienced the death of one of its children, Margaret felt that she should offer her staff the opportunity of training in bereavement care. She reflected sadly that it was after the event, and it was unlikely that they would experience the death of another child in the school—but who could say? According to the statistics, there would almost certainly be individual children bereaved after the death of a parent, grand-parent, sibling or friend. She felt that her staff had coped—just— and six weeks later they were still coping, more by intuition than knowledge, but they were by no means confident that they had met the children's needs adequately. Both she and her teachers wanted to be better prepared for the future.

Adele, the counsellor who had come into school the week Greg died, was more than happy to be approached by Margaret for this purpose. She was disappointed that the course she had set up specifically to help teachers understand child bereavement had not been taken up by many schools. She did recommend, however, that any training in one school should be opened out to other primary schools in the area. Then there could be a sharing of experiences about different kinds of bereavement, and perhaps mutual support in the future. She also felt that the course should be open to classroom assistants and midday supervisors who were interested.

There was quite a good response from the other schools. Thirty-five teachers and assistants assembled in the Hillside School hall and Margaret was pleased to see that all of her staff were there.

THE ROLE OF TEACHERS IN MEETING THE NEEDS OF BEREAVED CHILDREN

Adele began by addressing the teachers in a very direct way. 'I am sure you can understand how parents and families may be too upset by the death of one of their members to support their children adequately, or even respond to their needs. So—who are the next most trusted adults they know? You teachers and school helpers. And after the home, which may have suddenly turned into a place of frightening insecurity and grief, where is the obvious familiar place in which the children can find normality and predictable behaviour? Your schools, with their structure and routine.

'You know each child individually. You know your classes, how the children in them relate and react and work together. You know that children need help in expressing their feelings and needs, especially the younger ones, and you have the experience and materials to help them do this appropriately. The PSHE guidelines suggest that this is part of your job anyway. You have learned that children can only accept what they are capable of taking in or dealing with at the time; and if they react with anti-social behaviour and are generally unco-operative, or even aggressive towards you, you know not to take it personally.

'All the research shows that young children are helped most in their bereavement by trusted adults whom they know well and with whom they feel safe. You can be those adults whom the children trust and turn to with questions that are bothering them. School can be a real haven in a world that has become so frightening and disordered.'

Everyone began to feel more comfortable, even quite good about themselves. They were the experts after all. They just needed a bit of training.

'It doesn't look as if she'll make us do any of those dreadful role-plays,' whispered Carole to her neighbour.

'I'm all right as long as we don't have to talk about our own experiences,' her neighbour replied.

Adele continued, 'I wanted to start with the important place that teachers and schools can have in the lives of children who are experiencing bereavement. Now you tell me what you want from today—the issues that you would like us to look at.'

WHAT THE TEACHERS WANTED FROM THE TRAINING DAY

The group had no hesitation about telling her what they wanted.

'I want to be able to answer the children's questions.'

'How do you explain what happens after death?'

'What about children of different faiths?'

'I want to know what kind of behaviour to expect from children who have just lost a parent or grandparent.'

'Can you tell us about the different kinds of behaviour of children at different key stages?'

'How much time should we give to one bereaved child when there are 29 others who need to be getting on with their work?'

'What can we do in this kind of situation?'

❖

'OK. I'm going to begin with three headings and see if they cover what you are asking.' Adele began to write on a flipchart.

- The reactions of children to bereavement at different key stages
- Responding constructively to these reactions
- Issues about life after death for different faiths

'Do you think those headings cover the issues you've mentioned?' asked Adele. There was a general assent. 'Nothing else?' Silence.

Adele thought for a moment. No one had mentioned children's feelings. She hoped that this would come out in the course of the morning.

'We'll start with the first two themes. How many of you have had experience of children who have been bereaved?' About two-thirds of the group put up their hands.

'Right. Will you divide into three groups according to the key stage you are teaching—Foundation and Key Stage 1, lower Key Stage 2, and upper Key Stage 2—and write down on these sheets of paper any reactions you have noticed in your children. Please will one person from each group write, and then feed back to the group as a whole. OK? You've got half an hour from now.'

Everyone settled down to the exercise. Nearly everyone had something to say. When they were together again, Lorraine started the feedback with the reactions of the youngest classes.

REACTIONS TO BEREAVEMENT: FOUNDATION AND KEY STAGE 1

'We had to make a distinction between a whole class reacting to the death of one person, and an individual child reacting to a personal bereavement,' said Lorraine. 'My whole class was affected by the death of Greg and everyone was asking lots of questions. But when Ellie, Greg's sister, came back, the class wasn't nearly so forth-coming, and we ended up reacting to her.'

'That's a good distinction,' said Adele. 'So your handling of it was different, according to whether the child who was bereaved was in the class. Ellie was obviously more affected at a personal level by losing her brother, and needed individual attention, and the class was more affected generally by the subject of death and wanted to ask questions.'

She looked at the sheet of paper Lorraine was holding. 'Do you think you could feed back the class reactions and individual reactions separately? It would be helpful for the rest of us.'

'I'll try,' said Lorraine, looking at her sheet of paper.

CLASS REACTIONS

- Questions about the person who has died: where are they now? What will they be wearing or doing? Will they be happy?
- Questions about heaven: where is it, what is it like, will other people be there, who will look after them?
- Expressions of fear—of monsters, of the dark.
- General anxiety and insecurity.

INDIVIDUAL REACTIONS

- Clinging to adults, especially classroom and lunchtime assistants.
- Great anxiety about small things—afraid of being on their own, even going to the toilet on their own, anxious about being met after school.
- Frequent complaints of tummy aches and 'hurts'.
- Regression to thumb sucking, occasional toilet accidents, tears over trivial incidents.
- Being upset one minute, then laughing and shouting with the others as if everything was normal.
- Hyperactivity, inability to concentrate, chattering non-stop, constant fidgeting.
- Sudden flopping, looking tired and withdrawing from others.
- Finding something soft to hold.
- Occasional statements that the dead person is close by and happy.
- Talking as if the person who has died is still alive, or assuming that they will come back.

❖

'You've given us a lot of reactions. Well done,' said Adele. 'Would you say that you needed knowledge and information to cope with the class, and more awareness of feelings for the child who was individually bereaved?'

'Yes, I think that's right,' said Pam, a teaching assistant. 'But we didn't know what Ellie was feeling. She was obviously troubled, but she didn't say why.'

'She probably couldn't say why,' said Adele. 'Five-year-olds don't know why they feel as they do. It comes out in behaviour. Can anyone from this group tell us something you did with the class as a whole, that seemed to be positive?'

'Group activities rather than work on their own,' said someone.

'Such as...?'

'Singing favourite songs, listening together to stories.' Lorraine told them about the Circle Time and acting out the caterpillar-to-butterfly story. Others mentioned both noisy and quiet games.

'Doing things together like that does seem to be both calming and strengthening,' said Adele. 'And what about the individual child like Ellie? How did she fit into these activities?'

'She didn't seem to stay with us unless we were talking about her,' said Lorraine.

'We tried to cope together but eventually I had to ask Pam to take her into the comfy corner for a while. I had to do that for several days, and still do when she seems disturbed.'

'That is probably what she needs,' said Adele. 'You might not find out what is in her mind, but you can help her feel valued, safe and secure and cared for.'

THEORY BEHIND THE REACTIONS: FOUNDATION
AND KEY STAGE 1

'Five- and six-year-olds are particularly vulnerable to any change in what they have known as a safe world up to now, so they cling to adults who represent safety. Then, because they are only just emerging from the self-centred stage of thinking—the belief that the world revolves round them—their main concern at first may be "Who will look after me if a parent has died, or if parents are preoccupied with grief?" That creates a lot of anxiety, and will come out in demanding, attention-seeking behaviour.

'For the same reason, they often have an irrational sense of guilt that somehow they might have caused the death—perhaps because of something they said or thought. Conversely, they might think that they can bring the person back to life by wishing it hard enough. They won't articulate these beliefs, and it may be a very heavy burden of guilt or responsibility on their small shoulders.

'A five-year-old may tend to deny the death as a kind of defence against pain they can't cope with. They may also try to deny the finality of death, and they will not be able to stand grieving for as long at a time as older children. They will suddenly change to behaving as if everything is normal, or throwing themselves into play. Some adults may think they don't care, whereas nothing is further from the truth.

'There are a number of books about young children who have lost someone close to them. Introducing these tactfully, and reading them with the child, may help him or her to identify what they are feeling, so that they don't feel so alone with their thoughts, whether or not they say anything.'

REACTIONS TO BEREAVEMENT: LOWER KEY STAGE 2

After some discussion, Adele asked, 'Now what about the lower Key Stage 2 children? What have you got on your sheet?'

Carole stood up.

'We've got most of the same things—irrational fears of monsters and fires, hyperactivity, clinging to parents before school and to other adults, regression to temper tantrums or picking fights with other children, behaving normally one minute and bursting into tears the next, lack of concentration and general restlessness, fear of being alone.'

'Yes, and can you divide the children's reactions into class and individual?'

'Some of us did,' said Carole. 'I couldn't because my class as a whole were all personally affected by the death of Greg, though some felt it more than others. My group thought it would be useful to concentrate on coping with a whole class. I am finding it difficult to keep breaking off lessons to answer more questions, but it seems necessary. There's no point in waiting until it's a convenient time for me.'

'No, that's right,' agreed Adele. 'What else have your group written down?'

Carole read out from her sheet.

- A sort of lack of trust in the normal processes of life; anxiety, the feeling that life isn't safe any more.
- Again, illness and aches and pains, but there's also a sense of panic about things like 'what would happen if they couldn't breathe any more'.
- A dawning awareness that they, or someone close to them, could die.
- Anger, but they don't seem to know why they feel angry.
- Attention-seeking behaviour—but it doesn't seem right to punish them.
- They're obsessed by what happens to the body after death, and have weird ideas about afterlife. They ask questions every day about this. They want to know exactly what happens when people die. One boy said his mum said there was no such thing as life after death—which was quite unsettling to the others.
- Withdrawal to a corner, as if it's too much to cope with.

'Thank you,' said Adele. 'So your children seem to have a lot of the same feelings as the younger ones, but they are more intense, or they ask more questions to clarify issues. There's a higher level of understanding, or seeking to understand the process of death and beyond. Some are aware of their own mortality and can't face it at this stage.

'You're very wise, Carole, to break off from normal lessons if the level of anxiety is high—as long as you can get them back to their work soon afterward. And I suppose you let individuals who are upset or unsettled leave the class for a short time and go with the assistant, do you?'

'Most days,' said Carole, 'though not so often now. We actually made part of the storeroom into a quiet place. It's been well worth it.'

'Good. Have you found any class activities that seem to help?'

'Yes, we've played music games, and even done a sort of dance-drama to express feelings of fear and anger, pretending to be lions and tigers.'

'We organized games in the playground,' said a classroom assistant, 'and we keep an eye on any child on their own who seems upset.'

'That's so important,' said Adele. 'Unstructured times like play-time and dinnertime can be quite frightening to those who are feeling insecure or vulnerable.

'Now, what about the older children? Have you got different things on your list?'

REACTIONS TO BEREAVEMENT: UPPER KEY STAGE 2

Alan stood up. 'We've got more changes in behaviour than the others, but probably the same feelings underneath.'

CLASS REACTIONS

- Insecurity, states of high anxiety about floods, earthquakes, serial killers on the loose, hospitals, and illness generally.
- Preoccupation with danger—awareness that accidents can and do happen even when care is taken.

- Mood swings. One moment they are in high spirits, and the next they are very bad-tempered.
- Withdrawal to a corner, or within their own world. They get left behind in their work as they can't seem to concentrate for more than a few minutes.

Alan stopped for a moment and began to comment on what he had written.

'We talked about the differences between the boys and the girls who are going through bereavement. Obviously we can't generalize about that, but the boys can become very aggressive in the playground and fight and swear, and they can be uncommunicative in class—disobedient too, as if they've not heard, and they will take pains to cover up their feelings if they can manage it. They want to appear normal, to fit in with their peer group, and they definitely do not want to be seen crying. Two of us have experienced boys stealing.

'The girls tend to cry with friends and let themselves be comforted, and they will talk more if we get them on their own. It helps if they have a special friend.

'There is a tendency for both boys and girls to be hypersensitive and to feel misunderstood and rejected.'

THEORY BEHIND THE REACTIONS: KEY STAGE 2

'Thank you, Alan.' Adele blu-tacked the three sheets on the wall. 'Can you see? The same emotions and feelings are coming up for all children, and, depending on their age and stage of development, it comes out in different kinds of behaviour. But just like adults, children are quite unprepared for the mass of overwhelming emotions that come upon them at times of bereavement. The older ones may have more understanding of death, but all children need help in expressing how they feel, in their own way and in a safe environment. It's the beginning of the way to dealing with bereavement. The rest will follow if the emotional channels are unblocked.

'You all mentioned either fear of monsters or fear of the dark. This happens particularly when children cannot find the reassurance they need. It is likely to stop when they have accepted the death and had their questions answered, and when they feel safe with people they trust.

'There may be a turnaround in the behaviour of normally well-behaved children if they are trying to be specially good at home and doing what is expected of them.

'You see, there is a sense in which all children, whatever their age, feel the same sense of loss, pain and confusing emotions that adults do. They may all experience shock, disbelief, numbness, despair, anger, guilt, anxiety and fear, and they will react according to their stage of development.

'The younger ones cannot describe their feelings. They don't even know what it is they are feeling—they just feel generally insecure, afraid, confused and distressed. A teacher or assistant who is firm, consistent and warm can help them to feel that the world is still all right.

'A class which has been bereaved will be full of children feeling the loss, and may well be helped and guided together. If it's one child in the class, you will still need to know how they are likely to react, and help them accordingly—but in a more personal, private way, with the help of assistants. Stories and poetry are very effective ways of helping children identify their feelings and discuss them. I'll finish this session by reading a poem written by a friend of mine, about a child whose grandfather had died.'

WHEN GRANDAD DIED

Everybody cried, and I did too, but I didn't quite know why...
Everything seemed different at home,
and nobody wanted to play any more.
And people got cross, and shouted, and it always felt like my fault...
But it wasn't.

And I wanted to see Grandad, but they said I couldn't
And I cried and they cried
But I still didn't quite know why...

I went to school, and worked and played
And for a while everything felt better.
But it wasn't.

'Tomorrow,' I thought, 'it'll be OK, and the tears will stop,
and the other people will go away,
and Grandad will come back.'
But he didn't.

'He's dead,' they said, over and over...
'He can't come back.'

But I didn't know why... and they wouldn't tell me.

'Where has he gone?' I wanted to know
'He's gone to heaven to be with God,' they said...
'Jesus is looking after him now.'

So I told them I could look after him here, but they wouldn't listen.

So the days went by,
And it was my birthday... and it was Christmas...
and still Grandad didn't come back.

Perhaps they were right, perhaps he couldn't.
And then I began to remember the things that Grandad had told me
About living and about dying.

'We can't live for ever,' he would say…
'Our bodies would get so tired.

But the inside part of us,
The part that loves and cares and thinks and dreams…
That part doesn't die,

It lives on, in heaven with God.
We are given a new body, one that will never die.
And heaven is wonderful,' said Grandad,
'Full of light and beauty and colour and happiness.'

'Jesus promised,' Grandad told me, 'he would be with us
For ever and ever and ever…
And Jesus always keeps his promises,' said Grandad.

And all my thinking made me cry
And I began to understand why…

And I miss my Grandad, and I wish he was here.
But I know he is safe
And I can think about him, and talk to God about him
And remember him.

And in heaven, where nothing and nobody ever dies,
God is holding my Grandad as he holds us all…
In his love
For ever and ever and ever…

BY RUTH BRIDGES

CHECKPOINTS

- Children go through an emotional grief process similar to that of adults but lack the understanding and experience to be able 'to recognize, name and deal with their feelings in a positive way' (National Curriculum PSHE guidelines).
- Teachers, classroom assistants and other helpers have an important role in enabling children to say what they feel like, in showing that they accept these feelings, and in helping them to express them in an appropriate way.
- Since parents may not be able to support their children because of their own grief, teachers are often the most available, suited people to take on this task, as trusted adults who know and understand their children in the secure, stable school environment.

---- *Chapter 7* ----

THE TRAINING DAY CONTINUES

Adele, the leader of the training day, had found out from the teachers and classroom assistants what they wanted from the day, and the morning had mainly been spent looking at the reactions of children who had been bereaved and the theory behind these reactions.

Adele now wanted the teachers to look at their own feelings and experiences of bereavement. They would never be confident to answer the children's challenging questions about death unless they themselves felt reasonably sorted out about it. Adele wanted them to think about how it feels to be an eight-year-old, for example, going back to school after the death of a family member.

PERSONAL EXPERIENCES OF BEREAVEMENT

'What I would like you to do now is to look at any bereavements or significant losses you have experienced in your own lives, and to see how well-understood you felt by other people at the time, whether or not you were able to express how you were feeling, whether people were prepared to listen—and whether there is still deep pain inside you whenever you think about the one who has died.'

Adele saw some of them grimacing and smiled. 'I'm sorry, but it really is essential to your helping children effectively. You may have very unhappy feelings about someone dying when you were a child. Perhaps no one explained things to you and you were left feeling confused, frightened or angry. Perhaps you were not included in the funeral and felt that your feelings were not considered. Or you may have had a more recent experience that affected you deeply, and there was no one you could talk to about how you felt who seemed to understand. So you were left with strong feelings like guilt or anger or pain which had no outlet.

'You may not have realized that it was perfectly normal to be feeling like you did. These kinds of feelings, if they are not resolved at the time, can come to the surface when you are faced with another death, and can make you want to avoid helping others to deal with it. It brings the pain back. Do you understand what I am getting at?'

There was no response except from Frances, who nodded enthusiastically. Adele went on, 'Well—those who really can't bear the idea of looking at their own experiences could go and look at the books over there. And if you think that you have absolutely no experience of death, even that of a pet, you will still have experiences of some kind of personal, painful loss such as moving house, divorce, or being abandoned by a friend.

'I'm going to ask you to find one other person—it might be someone you know and trust, or you might prefer someone you don't know. Spend about ten minutes each, sharing any experience of death or loss that has hit you, how you felt, and whether you were able to express your feelings to anyone. Will the "listener" allow the other to talk without interrupting, and convey that you are listening by your facial expression and the occasional nod? Off you go.'

Everyone except two settled down to sharing their experiences. Adele noticed one woman becoming visibly upset and went over to her quickly. 'Would you like to talk to my colleague in the room next door?'

'No, I've started now and I think I want to go on,' replied the woman. 'I've never really cried about my father before.'

Adele let them go on for half an hour, then said, 'There are some deep feelings, aren't there? I really am sorry if this exercise brought back painful feelings which you would rather forget. If you would like to talk some more about your own personal bereavements, please do let me know after the session is over. Alternatively, you may prefer to talk to a friend.

'When you were listening, was it difficult to restrain yourselves from interrupting, or chipping in with your own experiences? And when you were talking, did you really feel that you were being listened to and that your feelings were accepted without judgment?'

THE ART OF LISTENING

'Listening is a skill that teachers in particular may need to work at,' said Adele. 'Teachers are good talkers—you have to be—but there is a danger that you can lose the art of listening.

'I can tell you in general about the reactions of children to bereavement, I can help you to understand the process, and I can give you ideas about what you can do. But the most valuable thing you can do to help children who are bereaved is to give time and space and opportunities to listen to the child—how each one uniquely feels about their loss, what questions they feel they need to ask, what they want to do. Then, and only then, can you acknowledge their particular pain, maybe give them the particular assurance that they need and enable them to feel valued where they are.

'You had a taste of listening and being listened to just then, but if you would like to learn more about it, do enrol on the Listening Course that these leaflets tell you about. It's one of the first steps to the healing of all the pain and hurt or angry emotions that most people feel after a close bereavement.'

ROLE-PLAY: AN EIGHT-YEAR-OLD CHILD WHO HAS LOST A PARENT RETURNS TO SCHOOL

'I'd like to do something quite different now,' said Adele. 'Suppose you are confronted one morning by a child who has returned to school after the death of a family member—which is quite likely to happen. That child may not immediately show the kind of behaviour or reactions we have been talking about, but might be unusually disruptive or withdrawn. How do you know what that child is feeling? What will you say or do?'

They all looked at her expectantly. Adele continued, slowly, 'At the risk of becoming even more unpopular, I'm going to ask you to be a class of eight-year-olds, first thing in the morning when you've just gone into the classroom. I'd like one of you to be the teacher, one to be the classroom assistant—and one of you to be the child.'

'Not a role-play,' groaned one teacher.

Adele laughed. 'Well, sort of. But don't worry, I'll take you through it, and most of you probably won't need to say anything. Will anyone volunteer to be the child?'

There was a long silence. Then Carole's classroom assistant, Joan, spoke up hesitantly. 'I will if no one else will. Actually, I was in that position. My mother died when I was eight, and everyone at school just went on as if nothing had happened. My teacher never said anything.'

'Thank you… Joan, is it? Can you remember just how you felt as that eight-year-old?'

Joan thought. 'I felt I wasn't the same as I had been before—and I felt different from the others. In fact, I felt as if I had a disease.'

'Right. Now will the rest of you get the tables set up, and sit at them as the children in Joan's class. Put one table at the front for your teacher. Who'll be Joan's teacher?'

Carole volunteered, more to support Joan than anything else.

'We need a classroom assistant too,' said Adele, 'and maybe another child—Joan's friend.' One of the other assistants and one of the teachers volunteered. Adele took them out and gave them a couple of scenarios in the school day, then left them for a while to discuss what they would say. When they came back in, Carole went to the teacher's table at the front while Joan and her friend sat at the empty table. The classroom assistant sorted things out at the side of the room.

'The scene is set,' said Adele. 'Who's going to start?'

Teacher: It's good to have you back with us, Joan. We've been thinking about you over the last few days, haven't we, children? And we're all very sorry about your mum. Is there anything you'd like to tell us before we tell you what we've been doing?

Joan shakes her head.

Teacher: *(To the class)* We'll go on with the ancient Egyptians. Mrs Parry, will you give out the worksheets we were doing yesterday? I'd like you all to turn to the second sheet, on Egyptian hieroglyphics. When you've finished, I'm going to ask you what a hieroglyphic is. While you're doing that, I'm going to help Joan catch up with what she's missed.

Carole goes to sit by Joan and points things out to her from a book. Then she gives her the first worksheet.

Teacher: Start with the pyramids and if you need any help, just ask, and I'll be with you. And Joan, if you get stuck or don't want to do it any more, let me know, won't you? You can go any time you like into the quiet corner with Mrs Parry.

Joan starts on her work. The class continues with their worksheets.

Adele stood up. 'It's nearly playtime now. Carole, you might need to say something before you go off for your coffee.'

Teacher: *(Going over to Joan)* Are you all right going out to play with the others? You can stay with Mrs Parry in the classroom if you like.
Joan: I want to be with Becky and Izzie. It's been boring at home on my own.

The whole class go out.

Adele came forward again. 'Morning school goes on, much as usual. Carole notices that Joan is doodling instead of writing, but isn't asking for any attention and seems all right. But after the lunch break, when Carole comes into her classroom before afternoon school, she finds Mrs Parry there with Izzie and Joan. Izzie is crying. Will the four of you take your places in the empty classroom, please.'

Assistant: Izzie's a bit upset, Mrs Carole, so I brought her in, with Joan.

Teacher: What is it, Izzie? What's the matter?

Izzie: *(Sniffing)* It's Joan. She's being horrid to me.

Joan: No, I'm not. She kept asking stupid questions. I wanted to play with Becky as well, but Becky didn't want to play with me and Izzie kept asking me what my mum looked like when she was dead.

Izzie: I didn't. I just wanted to know what it was like having a dead mum.

Teacher: That's a natural question, but maybe Joan doesn't want to tell you because it's upsetting for her. Joan, if people ask you questions that you don't want to answer, what could you say?

Joan: I'd say I don't want to talk about it.

Teacher: Go on, then.

Joan: I just don't want to talk about it, Izzie.

Izzie: That's all right. I just wanted to know what dead people looked like, that's all.

Teacher: What do you say, Joan?

Joan: *(Shouts)* Izzie, I don't want to talk about it... Well, she looked sort of white and not real.

Izzie: You'd rather have me than Becky, wouldn't you?

Joan: No, I want Becky as well.

Teacher: Perhaps Becky doesn't understand how you are feeling, Joan. Now why don't you two give out these books for me before the others come in?

'All right,' said Adele. 'We'll leave it there for the moment. How are you feeling, Joan?'

'Not very good, really,' said Joan. 'I was looking forward to going back to school and being with my friends—but they didn't seem like my friends any more. They were different—or I was different.'

'That's right. You would have changed. You couldn't go back to where you were before. People often lose their old friends after a bereavement and make new ones. How did you feel when you first arrived?'

'I was glad everyone knew, and I was glad the teacher mentioned my mum. That was all she needed to say. And she came to me and helped me catch up with the others. It felt good to work again. It was normal and I began to feel more like the others. Oh, and I liked the way she asked me if I'd like to say something. I didn't but I might have done. It made me feel more in control of things than I had since Mum was so ill.'

'Goodness knows what happened at playtime,' said Adele. 'That's where everything can fall apart, though it's often good for the child to play freely. How do you feel, Izzie?'

'A bit confused. I wanted to be Joan's special friend and somehow I'd got it wrong. I think Becky had the right idea.'

'Friends do need support,' said Adele. 'It can be too much for them. You handled it beautifully as the teacher, Carole, but you might also write a note to Izzie's parents to let them know that she was hurt and might need extra support. I especially liked the way you helped Joan tackle questions she didn't want to answer.

'What about you, Mrs Parry? You did a good job with the two girls.'

'I could see how important it was to keep an eye on children who are upset. I was looking out for Joan being upset but not her friends. I wouldn't have done anything about it if Joan hadn't been with Izzie. Actually, I'm sorry there wasn't time for more. I was looking forward to taking Joan out of the classroom situation and into the quiet corner.'

'You might not have to,' said Adele. 'Or it might come in the next few days or even weeks. Little things like someone talking about their mum, or birthdays or Mother's Day, will trigger off memories and tears.

'Well, thank you for taking part. Are you coming out of role now? Joan, where does this leave you?'

'I'm grown-up again—it's all right,' said Joan. 'I suppose I feel a bit sad that it wasn't like that for me all those years ago, but it makes me all the more determined to keep a close eye on any child who could be upset.'

LIFE AFTER DEATH: THE BODY AND THE SPIRIT

'You asked for a session about the concept of life after death, taking into account the beliefs of different faiths,' said Adele. 'I'd like to do this in story form. This is probably more suitable for the older children, but I'm sure you can adapt it for the younger ones. Make yourselves comfortable, sit on a cushion if you like, and I'll begin.

'Ever since human life began on this earth, every single person has been born with a body, which can be seen, and a soul or spirit, which cannot be seen.

'The body is the outside part of us which is suited to life on earth. Our bodies have legs to walk, hands to do all kinds of things, eyes to see, and ears to hear. They have a digestive system to deal with food, lungs to breathe in the air, a brain to think with and, most important, a heart to pump the blood around and keep all the other parts working.

'The soul, or spirit, is the inside part of us which leads us to love people, which draws us to beautiful things like flowers and poetry, music and painting. Sometimes the spirit inspires us to write poetry ourselves, or compose music or paint beautiful pictures, and sometimes the spirit makes us aware of God and makes us want to know him better.

'We cannot see or touch our spirit, but we know it is there—a very important part of each one of us.

'Now, as we all know, the body does not live for ever. Sometimes it becomes too old and tired to work properly. Legs get weak and can't walk easily; hands get painful joints and can't move without hurting. Eyes can't see so well and ears can't hear. And when the heart gets tired of pumping the blood around, the body stops working altogether. The body dies because it has become worn out with age.

'Sometimes the body dies before it gets old. Sometimes it has an accident and is too damaged to work. Sometimes it has an illness that cannot be cured and stops the body from working. Most bodies recover from accidents and from illness, but sometimes they die.

'Now, remember that the body is only one part of us—the outside part. The special inside part of us, the spirit, that loves people and beautiful things, and inspires us to create beautiful things, and makes us aware of God—that part of us never, never dies. Our spirit leaves our body when we die, and goes on to live for ever and ever.

'You may ask, "Where do our spirits live? Where do they go to?" People of different religions have slightly different answers to this.

'Christians say that when someone dies, their spirit is looked after by Jesus and may go on with him to heaven. They say that God gives our spirit a new body which will be suited to life in heaven. The Bible says that heaven is very beautiful, filled with light and love, where Jesus and God are with us for ever and ever.

'Muslims say that when someone dies, their spirit is looked after by an angel for a short time and may go on to Paradise, which is very beautiful.

'Jews say that the spirit goes on to a special spiritual world which they call "the world to come".

'Hindus say that when someone dies, their spirit sheds the body and may go into another body. Then when that body dies, the spirit will go into another. This may happen several times until finally the spirit reaches God, or Brahman, as they call him.

'Some Chinese people say that when someone dies, their spirit crosses a bridge between this life and the next life to join all their ancestors in heaven.

'So, although people of different religions believe different things about what happens to the spirit, they all believe that the spirit separates from the body at death and goes on to live a new kind of life.

'There are some people who say that they do not know whether or not they believe in God or heaven. They sometimes say that when someone dies, their spirit lives on in the beautiful things that the person loved—perhaps in gardens or by lakes or mountains or in the people they loved.

'You may ask: what happens to the body that has died? Does it go anywhere too? No, the body cannot do anything or go anywhere because it doesn't work any more. It doesn't move or see or hear. It doesn't eat or breathe or think. It doesn't feel anything—the heat or the cold, or pain. It is just an outside shell, like the skin that a snake casts off.

'So the body is buried in the ground or burnt in a fire, at a special ceremony called a funeral. The people who knew and loved the person who has died all meet together at the funeral to remember the person and to say their goodbyes. They comfort each other because they are sad that they are separated from the one who has died. As time goes on, they still miss the person but they remember the happy times they had together and all that was special about them. And they are glad that the person is still alive in a new kind of way, and will never die now, but will live for ever and ever.'

WHAT TEACHERS CAN DO TO HELP CHILDREN WHO HAVE BEEN BEREAVED

'Our final session must be: what can you do at school to help children who have been bereaved?' Adele turned on the OHP and pointed to the first heading, which was about feelings.

FEELINGS: HELPING TO IDENTIFY THEM
WHEN CHILDREN ARE DISTURBED

Ask the children what they feel like inside. Here are some possible answers.

- Like a bear or a tiger—angry
- Like screaming or yelling loudly—frustrated or angry
- Like crying or curling up in a corner—sad
- Scared of being alone or in the dark—insecure, frightened
- Like there's a big hole in their tummy that hurts—yearning, hurting

Don't try to distract the children: accept their feelings. If they say they don't know how they feel, try reading a story or poem about a child or animal who has lost someone close. Ask if it's like that for them. See if they can write their own story or poem.

FEELINGS: HELPING TO EXPRESS THEM

Anger: Leap around growling or roaring like an angry tiger. It might be helpful to take the children outside for this activity.

Frustration: Draw a picture of a volcano in vivid reds, yellows and blacks, or act out the eruption of a volcano.

Sadness: Could the children draw that sad feeling? Alternatively, curl up in a corner with a soft toy and listen to some sad music, or dance or sing to the music.

Fear: Ask the children when they feel scared; then repeat it out loud while staying close to them and discuss together how you can tell the fear to go. The power of the fear will have been reduced by naming it, and by facing it together the child should receive the reassurance that is needed.

Yearning: The child may like to talk or write, or draw some
            memory of the one who has died and keep it in a safe
            place.

These are only examples of ways to express feelings. Children
usually have their own ideas about what they would like to do.

PROVIDING ALTERNATIVES TO TEACHER AND CLASSROOM

Try to appoint one caring adult, like a classroom assistant or helper,
as an anchor for a particular child, to be there when needed.

Try to set up a quiet place or room, with soft toys, cushions,
books and play materials, to which a upset child can retreat with an
adult, to cry, express feelings, or ask questions.

REMEMBERING SPECIAL OCCASIONS

Be alert to times like birthdays, anniversaries and Christmas. Discuss
with children what rituals they would like to use to mark the
occasion. For example:

- Make a gift and put it in a special place with flowers, or on the
  grave.
- Write a letter or birthday card and put it by a photograph.
- In a class bereavement, make a collage or album of the dead
  child's life at school, and have a memory box of their possessions
  and things the children want to remember about them.
- On Mother's Day or Father's Day, if the class are making cards or
  simple gifts, ask any children who have lost a parent if they would
  like to make a picture of that person and/or make a card for the
  person who is caring for them now.

VISIT TO CHILD'S HOME

A personal visit is likely to be appreciated by parents and children alike.

Ask parents and children if it would be all right if you came to the funeral, perhaps with one or two of their friends. This opens the way for further contact with parents.

EDUCATION ABOUT DEATH

If the bereaved child is absent, take the opportunity to talk to the rest of the class about the subject of death, answer questions, and discuss the feelings it brings up and the need for support.

Encourage the children to support the bereaved child—for example, by making sure the bereaved child is not left on his or her own in the playground or without a partner in some activity, and by making sure the child is invited to other people's homes to play.

WORKING TOWARDS A MEMORIAL

Organize activities to generate funds for a memorial—for example, a school or class sponsored walk, concert, display, non-school uniform day and so on.

SUPPORT FOR YOURSELVES

Find support from each other in the staff room, and from friends who will listen to you.

❖

There were not many questions after this. Everyone seemed tired, some were emotionally drained and Adele ended the training day by thanking them all for being so ready to learn about the effects of bereavement on children of primary school age. 'How you respond now will have an influence on the rest of their lives—how they handle future loss and death, how they handle their own lives, and how they think about their own dying.'

CHECKPOINTS

- In describing what happens after death, all the main religions teach that there is a separation of the spirit from the body at death and that the spirit lives on in a new kind of life.
- Keep an eye on unstructured times like playtime and the dinner break. Children can be particularly vulnerable at these times.
- Consider the needs of the friends of bereaved children. Check out how they feel and, if necessary, inform the parents so that they can give extra support.

Chapter 8

WHEN TO REFER ON

Until now, I have emphasized the point that the best people to help children who are bereaved are usually those adults whom the children know well and trust, and who are prepared to be alongside them and listen. Parents can do this if they are sufficiently removed from the death themselves, or if they can let their children share in the family grief appropriately, but this is hard for parents who may already have too much to bear. This is why teachers, church leaders, group leaders and other relatives can have an important role in supporting children in times of need. Research has shown that most young children do not welcome the idea of counsellors coming in from the outside, since the counsellors do not know the children or the person who has died.

There are exceptions, however. Although everyone's bereavement process will move forward and backward, there may be 'sticking points' beyond which a person cannot move. It is impossible to give a time limit to this process and children in particular may have to go back and address certain issues at different stages of their development, but there are some symptoms that need close attention.

As a general rule, if a bereaved child has uncharacteristically negative behaviour after several months, and if this behaviour seems to have set into a pattern, it may be time to consult the parents about referral to a specialist. Unwillingness to join in class activities, alienation from friends, aggression, stealing, bullying, refusal to co-operate or work, unidentifiable aches and pains, absence from school—all these kinds of behaviour may have to be tolerated for short spells. They will usually improve as the necessary assurance, love and attention is given, as questions are dealt with and fears addressed. If they persist, however, and become set patterns of behaviour, the child may need help to move on.

Ten-year-old Gareth had always seemed a reasonably straight-forward boy, with a few good friends, usually polite and co-operative, and participative in class. He had returned to school after his brother's death shaken, unable to concentrate for long and reluctant at first to join in the normal energetic games of his peers. His teacher, Alan, had expected something like this, but then Gareth's behaviour slowly began to deteriorate into withdrawal from the rest of the class, rudeness to teachers and unwillingness to do any work. When his absences from school became more and more prolonged, Alan went to see Margaret, the headteacher.

IT HAS GONE ON LONG ENOUGH

'He's away as much as he's here,' said Alan, 'and, quite frankly, I'm relieved when he's not here. He stands out like a sore thumb in the class and makes no attempt to catch up with his work. He's not going to cope with his SATS at this rate.'

'That is a bit worrying,' said Margaret. 'Having so much time off school, I mean. I wonder what's going on at home for him. Can you go on being patient, Alan? It's going to take Gareth time to adjust to the class again and his parents may take years to adjust to the family situation.'

'In that case, Gareth's going to need help in coping,' said Alan, unexpectedly firmly.

'His behaviour gets worse every time he comes back, and I'm pretty sure he's been stealing. It only happens when he comes back, and I don't like to accuse him. He doesn't even want to play football now and he was the best striker on the school team. Actually, Margaret, I think his parents are keeping him off deliberately. He can't go on like this—and I can't seem to help him.'

'I'll go and see his parents,' said Margaret.

CONSULTING PARENTS

The visit had not worked out well, though Margaret was glad she had been. Sue Mitchell would not have it that Gareth could be a problem at school. 'He's perfectly all right at home,' she said, adding meaningfully, 'and that's where you'd think he would have problems.'

'I'm glad he's all right at home,' said Margaret. 'It's just that he's been away from school rather a lot and he's finding it so hard to catch up on the work he's missed that he isn't trying any longer. And he doesn't join in games with his friends any more...'

'Gareth hasn't been at all well recently. He's needed to be off school.'

'Yes, but he's become very withdrawn—not at all like the Gareth we know. I'm wondering if he'd like to talk to someone about what he is feeling at school. He doesn't seem to want to talk to his teacher, or me.'

'What are you suggesting—a shrink?'

Margaret had thought of an educational psychologist, but changed tack quickly. 'Some of the staff have found it helpful talking things over with the counsellor who's been coming into school, and I wondered if Gareth might like to talk to her. He's obviously very troubled, as you'd expect, and he's hardly talking to anyone at school—or home, I gather?'

'I've just said—Gareth's no trouble at all at home. He's actually very helpful. Now if you were to suggest counselling for my husband, I might agree. He is being a problem...'

'Mmmm... well, that might not be a bad idea,' agreed Margaret. 'But anyway, would you agree to Gareth seeing the counsellor?'

'Oh, I don't know,' said Sue wearily. 'Why don't you ask him? He's old enough to know his own mind.'

Luckily, Gareth did not need persuading. 'Will it be in lesson time?' was all he asked.

COUNSELLING FOR GARETH

Gareth went out of Alan's numeracy hour quite cheerfully and up to Margaret's room. The first thing he saw there was a partly made-up model aeroplane on the table. 'Hey, is that a Tornado?'

'I don't know what it is, but it's waiting to be finished off,' said the lady who was with Margaret. 'I'm Adele, and you must be Gareth. Have you made up any model aeroplanes before?'

'Lots,' said Gareth. 'I do them with Dad... well, I used to... he's been too busy lately.'

'Well, I'm probably not as good as your dad, but I thought we might work on this one together while we talked,' said Adele. Margaret withdrew. Adele seemed to know what she was doing.

'You need that part next,' said Gareth. 'I think I know where it goes.' He was soon engrossed. He loved making models. They worked together for a while before Adele asked casually, 'Why is your dad busy? Is he doing lots at home?'

'No,' said Gareth. That was the only response Adele was able to get out of him that morning, apart from comments on the aeroplane. She did not mind. She was at least building up some sort of working relationship with him. At the end of the session she said, 'I'm going to leave this just as it is and we can go on with it another day. Friday all right?'

It took two more sessions to finish the plane. Gareth became quite excited when Adele suggested that they might paint it next time. 'Can I show it to Dad? He'd love this, and it might get him going again.'

'Sure,' said Adele. 'Let's paint it first, though.' Somehow she knew she might lose Gareth's confidence if she pushed now. If Gareth did not want to talk at this stage, then she was not going to try to make him.

But Gareth did begin to talk, when the plane was finished. They beamed at each other over the finished product—a gleaming silver Tornado, poised like a bird for flight.

'What do you want to do with it, Gareth?' asked Adele.

'I'd really like to give it to Dad,' said Gareth. 'It might make him happy again.' He sighed.

'Do you want to talk about your dad?' asked Adele quietly. 'I think I might know a bit what it's like for your dad and mum just now.'

'Did you have a boy who died?'

'No, but I know parents who have. It completely changes them.'

'It's changed my dad a lot. He's never there now, and I'm left with Mum. Not that there's anything wrong with that,' he added loyally, 'but she wants me there all the time and I think Dad should be there more. He is there sometimes, but…'

'What happens when your dad is there?'

'He comes in from the pub and Mum shouts at him and then they row and it's just awful. Then they don't talk to each other for ages. They talk to me instead and ask me to pass on what they say. Greg would hate that. We all used to be happy together…' He bit his lip.

'You know, other parents who have lost a child behave like that,' said Adele. 'They're both too upset by the death to help each other.'

'What about me? I'm upset too and no one helps me. I have to stay off school and go with Mum when she needs to go out, I have to go out every night for chips or pizzas for tea, and I even have to put Ellie to bed and stop her going downstairs, and I can't say "no" or Mum'll get more upset.' Gareth stopped for breath.

❖

'It feels like you're having to be grown-up and do what your parents usually do even though you're not grown-up. And you'd like to say "no" to your mum sometimes but don't. Does that make you feel angry, like it's just not fair?'

'Well... I just try to do what they say... I get angry when I go to bed sometimes.'

'What do you do?'

'Just cry. It's the only place I can. You can't cry at school. It's all so crazy.'

'No, it's not crazy at all,' said Adele. 'Everything you've said is perfectly normal. But it's very, very hard for all of you. Let's put it down as well as we can on paper and I think you'll see why you feel as you do.

'Could you draw a picture of your mum and your dad and you on one of these sheets of paper, and cut them out? Do it how you see them, big or little, how they look most of the time, and then put them and you on this dark sheet of paper. Make a picture of what it's like at home. And, Gareth, anything that you say or do in this room is completely private. I won't tell anyone what you say. OK? I'll be over there sorting out my papers.'

FINDING WAYS OF EXPRESSING THE PROBLEM

Gareth set to work. His cut-out father was big, with stooping shoulders and red eyes, coming away from a building with lots of bottles in it. 'That's the pub,' he explained when Adele looked over his shoulder. Then he cut out a door, bent the edge and sellotaped it so that it stood out, and put it in front of his father. On the other side of the door he drew a picture of a small woman lying down on a couch, covering her face with her hands. 'That's Mum. She won't let Dad through the door.'

'And what about you? Can you draw where you are?'

Gareth made a figure that was bigger than his mum and placed it by the door on his mother's side, with his hand on the door knob.

'I want to get out but I can't. And I'm talking through the keyhole, telling Dad what Mum's saying, and not telling Mum what Dad's saying because he's swearing.'

'What are you feeling like inside? Can you draw inside the figure that's you?'

Gareth drew a tiny picture of a child with a huge mouth and big fists and stamping feet, inside the bigger picture.

'That's the real me shouting off, raging away. But on the outside I look cool and no one knows—not even at school. I stay cool and don't talk to anyone. It's better like that.'

Adele wanted to cry herself and wondered how she could help him. He was in danger of alienating himself from other people and losing himself if he went on like this. 'It sometimes helps to do something with strong feelings like that,' she said. 'Can you think of a way to get that real you out, so you don't burst?'

'There isn't a way,' said Gareth flatly. 'I'd have to be a rocket and shoot up into the sky and explode...'

'...with coloured stars falling from the explosions,' finished Adele. She was beginning to see a way through. 'Why don't we buy a rocket, a big one, and stick that picture of you round the outside?'

'Then I can shoot up and explode in the sky,' shouted Gareth. 'With a huge bang and masses of stars.'

'We'll do it after school tomorrow,' said Adele.

❖

The next day, Adele was waiting for Gareth after school with the biggest rocket she had been able to buy at the garden centre, and a bottle. Very carefully, Gareth glued round the rocket and stuck on to it the picture of himself with the tiny picture of how he really felt inside. Then the two of them went out into the middle of the playground and Gareth put the stick of the rocket into the bottle.

'I'd better light it,' said Adele. 'Stand back.'

They watched as the end of the rocket glowed brighter and brighter, and just when it seemed that nothing was going to happen, it suddenly shot off into the sky with a loud whoosh, higher and higher, until it seemed to stop and explode into showers of stars—first red, then yellow, then green, each with a loud bang. Then nothing. Gareth just stood looking up into the sky. Eventually Adele said, 'Let's go in now. I'll make a drink for us both.'

❖

Gareth sat down at Margaret's table looking pale. Adele gave him a cup of tea and asked, 'How do you feel now?'

Gareth didn't answer, and Adele could see him struggling with tears. 'Sort of empty inside. I don't want to go home. Mum and Dad will be the same.' And he covered his face with his hands.

'You might be able to talk to them,' suggested Adele slowly.

'They wouldn't listen to me,' said Gareth. He looked up hopefully. 'Do you think they could come and see you?'

'We could ask them,' said Adele. 'If they came with you, you might be able to tell them what it's like for you. It's sometimes easier in front of someone else. But it's getting late. Would you like me to take you home now? I'm going your way.'

❖

Gareth pushed past his mother and ran upstairs. 'He's a bit upset,' explained Adele, 'but I think it's a good thing. He probably needed to cry.'

'What a pity,' said Sue Mitchell. 'He seemed to enjoy coming to you.'

'I think he's managed to get a load off his chest,' said Adele. She hesitated. 'If you or your husband wanted to come at any time and talk as Gareth has done, do feel free to give me a ring. Or you could come with Gareth. I think he would like that. I'll leave my card with you.'

FAMILY COUNSELLING

The Mitchells actually turned up at school for Gareth's next session with Adele—without an appointment. Margaret showed them into her room, and Adele welcomed them, though she wished she could have had prior notice. Neil Mitchell looked embarrassed. 'I hope you don't mind,' he said, 'but Gareth asked us to come. He keeps saying he wants to talk to us but only if you're there. Isn't that right, son?'

Gareth looked a bit embarrassed too.

'I didn't think they'd come,' he said to Adele.

'Well, here we all are,' said Adele more cheerfully than she felt. 'And yes, there are things Gareth needs to say that he finds difficult. Are you OK, Gareth?'

Gareth was silent. Sue smiled at him. 'You know you can say anything you like to me, Gareth. We're friends, aren't we? Even more since Greg died.'

'That's it, Mum. I can't be your friend all the time. I'd do anything else for you, Mum, but I can't be what you want me to be. I... I want to be at school and play, though I miss Greg too. You need Dad, not me.'

Sue set her lips in a tight line. 'I know, but your dad's not there for me. Are you, Neil? You're out at the pub all the time, enjoying yourself, aren't you? What do you have to say about that, Neil?'

Gareth looked at Adele appealingly and Adele motioned to Neil to speak. He looked uncomfortable but spoke calmly. 'Don't be ridiculous. I only go out for an hour or so in the evenings...'

'Oh, Neil!'

He continued, 'Maybe a bit longer. Why do you think I go, Sue? Because they understand at the Cat and Lion. There's always someone I can talk to and I feel better when I've been there. There's nothing for me at home any more. You won't talk to me; you won't even sleep with me. That's why I go out, if you really want to know.'

'There's me, Dad. I want you at home,' said Gareth.

'You're not the only bereaved father to stay away from home,' said Adele. 'Do you know that there's a horrifyingly high rate of marriage breakdown after a child in the family has died? And you can see why. The worst thing that could ever happen to parents has happened to you. Greg was your son—both of you equally—and you both have your own grief. But you'll show it in different ways. You, Sue, think that Neil isn't grieving because he goes out to the pub, but he says he talks to people there and feels better…'

'Well, actually, I do sometimes come in somewhat the worse for wear,' said Neil. 'The boys buy me beers because they think that will help.'

'And does it?'

'I suppose it takes the edge off at the time, but I only have to go back to it. No, it helps to just talk, and they seem to listen.'

Adele turned to Sue. 'Where do you find your support, Sue?'

'I don't. There isn't anyone for me. I've got to keep going because of the children. Gareth helps me a lot. He's been wonderful.'

'And Gareth is feeling that pressure, it seems…'

❖

It was Gareth who brought them to the turning point. 'Dad, Mum and I just want you home with us, don't we, Mum?'

'Preferably not reeking of beer all the time,' said his mother.

Neil stared. 'Do you really want me, Sue? I didn't think you did any more, especially when you moved into Ellie's room.'

'You daft bat, of course I want you home. But you'll have to stop going to the pub all night and every night.'

'And you'll have to stop shouting at me all the time.'

Gareth was still a bit nervous. 'Will you be all right on your own in the daytime, Mum, if Dad's there at night?'

Sue sighed. 'I suppose so. You must get back into a regular pattern at school if you want to. I might ask if they'll take me back at work part-time.'

❖

Adele watched the family out of the window, going down the school drive. At least they were talking to each other. She was glad they had agreed to see her again in a fortnight's time, on their own. They would still need help to understand and accept each other's way of grieving, and to try to support each other. Gareth would probably be all right for a while. She threw the empty model aeroplane box into the waste basket and noticed that it was a Tornado, as Gareth had said.

CHECKPOINTS

- Bereavement grief is usually a process that takes time—different amounts of time for different people. Although there will be natural movement forward and backward within the process, there may be sticking points for the child or adult, points at which an outside therapist may be able to help.
- These sticking points may be recognized as uncharacteristic, usually negative, kinds of behaviour which become a pattern. For example, aggression, stealing, withdrawal, alienation, excessive anxiety, persistent sickness and so on may cover an underlying cause.
- A therapist such as a child psychologist or bereavement counsellor may enable older children to recognize and accept their feelings and express them in an acceptable way, then look together at possible underlying causes and support them in finding a way through.
- Parents who are bereaved may need help in understanding and accepting each other's ways of grieving, in supporting each other as well as they can, and finding other supports outside the family so that they do not lean too heavily on older children.

Chapter 9

WHERE IS GOD IN SITUATIONS
LIKE FATAL ACCIDENTS?

At the heart of all suffering is the question to which there is no easy answer: if there is a God who is almighty, if there is a God who is love, then why does he allow people to suffer tragedies or die prematurely from accidents and disease? And where is God in the darkness afterwards?

I will have to hand over the task of addressing these issues to the Reverend Oliver MacKenzie, who was beginning to feel pushed into it by some of the people from his church. Margaret, Greg's headteacher, was the most persistent. 'Why didn't God prevent it from happening?' she would ask, again and again. 'Why did that car have to come the very second Greg went on to the road?' Others in the church were also questioning the motives and even the existence of God in the aftermath of Greg's death.

Oliver knew that he could not provide a direct answer to these questions and he was interested to note that neither did Jesus. Jesus got involved—he showed great compassion for those who suffered and he healed many people—but he never explained why these things could happen to people when God loved them so much. He once explained that a man's blindness was *not* because he or his parents had done anything wrong. It was not God's punishment. But instead of explaining why, Jesus got on with the job of healing him (John 9:1–7).

In the end, Oliver decided to hold a meeting for anyone who was asking these kinds of questions. While praying for guidance, he began to feel that he should do his explaining by way of a story. He himself had gained glimpses of understanding through the stories and parables that Jesus had told—and anyway, Oliver liked telling stories.

He decided to start with the story of creation in the book of Genesis, but told in his own words. This might help people to understand how God had intended the world to be. The story of human disobedience, he reflected, attempted to explain how the world became as it is today. Then he hoped to move on to the New Testament and explain how God sent Jesus to bring light into the darkness of the world (John 12:46).

Oliver was not complacent about his task. He arranged a motley assortment of comfortable chairs in a circle in his study, and when everyone had arrived he began.

THE STORY OF CREATION

Adapted from Genesis 1:1—2:4 and John 1:1–3

'Before the beginning, before the universe ever came into being, there was God, and God alone. Unknown and unknowable, God held within himself all creativity, all love, all truth—and all life.

'Then came the beginning, when God expressed his creativity through the Word. The Word was part of God but apart from him too. He was like an intimate friend. Together they embarked upon the great act of creation, and they were so much together that I will call them both God. God created the universe. He created plants and all living creatures, and after each stage of creation God looked at what he had made and saw that it was good.

'Then God created an even higher form of life. He created man and woman, to be like himself in some ways but not every way. He made them to know him and love him as he loved them, to be creative as he was creative, to be perfectly good as he was perfectly good. He made them to love and care for each other and to love and care for his world.

'*But* he did not give them all his wisdom and knowledge, for that would have been too much for them to bear. God wanted his children to be happy, loving, caring, but carefree too. He wanted them to choose to live as he wanted them to live because they loved him.

'Now, for a time, God and man and woman were very happy together. They talked and they laughed and they played with each other. Man and woman were completely open to God's joy and love and guidance. They delighted in God, in each other and in creation, and God delighted in them. For a time they remained true to God's image in them. They were whole. They were good. They were content.'

Oliver paused. 'Are there any questions at this stage?'

'Yes,' said Margaret. 'Were there no accidents and no tragedies in that world?'

'No,' said Oliver, 'because God protected them from anything bad happening to them.'

'Then why doesn't he protect us now?' asked Margaret angrily.

'Good question,' said Oliver. 'I'll go on with the story, and I think—I hope—you'll begin to see.'

THE STORY OF THE FIRST SIN: THE START OF HUMAN DISOBEDIENCE

Adapted from Genesis 3:1–13

'For a while, those first people, called Adam and Eve, lived happily together in the beautiful world God had created.

'Then, one day, everything changed. It happened like this.

'Adam and Eve were playing together happily in the shade of a particularly beautiful tree when Eve said to Adam, "Just look at that fruit! I can almost taste it!" Adam replied, "It's *the* tree, Eve. We can't. Remember what God said"—and they both chanted together, "You may eat the fruit from any tree in the garden, except the one that has the power to let you know the difference between right and wrong…" Then they both laughed. It was the only thing God told them not to do, but they didn't mind. They both adored God and they never dreamt of doing anything he asked them not to do—until that day. It was all the serpent's fault. Or was it?

'They had often seen the serpent in the garden. He seemed quite nice really. He sometimes had a wicked grin that made them smile. What they didn't know, however, was that the serpent actually embodied the very spirit of evil. He didn't look particularly evil, and he had very attractive green and black markings on his body.

'Now… the serpent had been trying to find a way of seducing Adam and Eve away from God, and over to him. He wanted power over them instead of God having all the power. Until now he had not been successful because they were so devoted to God that they just did what he told them to. However, when he saw Eve looking at the fruit of *the* tree, the serpent suddenly saw his chance. He slithered through the grass and lay sleepily beside Eve as she looked at the fruit hanging down from the branch, just asking to be picked.

'He listened and watched as she turned to Adam and said, "I wonder why God told us not to eat that fruit. It looks perfectly harmless to me."

'"Well, we can't, and that's that," said Adam firmly. "It'll be bad for us, perhaps change us in some way, and God likes us as we are. Come on, let's go and play somewhere else."

'The serpent wrapped himself round the tree and grinned at them. "Do you believe everything he says?"

'"Are you talking about God?" asked Eve. "Of course we believe what he says. He's our friend and we love him."

'"Yes, well, he's all right," said the serpent. "It's just that he thinks he's the only one who knows everything. Take that fruit, for instance…" They all looked at it… "Can you give me any reason why you shouldn't eat it… if you wanted to, that is?"

'"He knows it won't be good for us," said Adam. "And by the way, God does know everything."

'"Sure," smirked the serpent, "and he doesn't want you to know

116

as much as he does." He unwrapped himself from round the tree, slithered a bit closer and spoke in a conspiratorial whisper, "I'll tell you something you don't know. If you wanted—say, just as an example—to have a bite of something you fancy…" and his eyes looked up at the fruit, "… well, why not? That fruit will open your eyes. You will see things differently, and you will become as wise and powerful as God. That's why he doesn't want you to eat it. It will give you the freedom to do your own thing sometimes instead of asking him all the time. However… you're big enough to make up your own minds. Just thought I'd mention it…" and the serpent glided away to watch them from a distance, with an evil smile on his face.

'Eve could wait no longer. She reached out, picked the fruit and took a bite. "Mmm… I've never had anything like this before. Try it, Adam. You'll love it." Adam was all agog now. He took a bite, handed it back, and between them they finished it off.

'They looked at each other, expecting to laugh as usual and talk about how good the fruit had been. But they did not laugh. Adam looked at Eve, and instead of seeing a beautiful natural woman, he saw a provocative female figure. "Cover yourself up, Eve, you don't look decent without any clothes."

'Eve was offended. Then she looked at Adam. And instead of seeing a beautiful natural man, she saw a provocative male figure. "And what do you think you look like?" she asked. "Cover yourself up too!"'

HOW WE WANT GOD'S PROTECTION—
BUT ON OUR TERMS

'That,' said Oliver, 'is how man and woman first lost their innocence and their reverence for God, and chose to disobey him, tempted by the spirit of evil. And that is the story of the world today. We want God's protection, but we are not prepared to follow God's rules of life. It doesn't seem like disobedience at first, but we want to live in the world our way and so we have become self-centred rather than God-centred.'

'But surely God could still protect innocent children and those who want to be good,' said Margaret.

'I'm afraid the fact is that the system of doing things our way is firmly in place now and we are all caught up in the process,' answered Oliver a bit awkwardly. He could see Margaret's point, and wished it were so. 'God gave men and women the choice between living in complete dependence upon him and being protected by him, and living independently from God and doing things their way. And there has to be a price to pay for the decision they made.

'We can see how the richer, more powerful countries grow at the expense of poorer, weaker ones, creating an underclass of poor people all over the world. People are greedy and over-exploit the earth's resources, giving little consideration to our environment and future generations. And in our own everyday life, many of us strive for power in our jobs, in our relationships, and even in our families sometimes. And those without power may become victims of the system.'

'I can see all that,' said Margaret. 'But where does Greg and what happened to him come into all this?'

Oliver sighed and tried to explain. 'You see, Greg and the car that killed him were, if I can put it this way, also victims of the system. We all want powerful motor cars to get us quickly and comfortably from one place to another. But if we are sometimes too tired or distracted to notice that there is ice on the roads, or that a child is coming too quickly round a corner and on to the road, there is no magic wand to stop the child going into the car.

'We want to buy our children exciting presents like roller-blades, but we don't take the trouble to build safe places for them to play on them, so they go on the pavements. God has let us get on with living the way we want and, whether we like it or not, he is not into magic ways of stopping us from having accidents.'

'So God has abandoned us and doesn't protect us, and it's all pretty hopeless, isn't it?' said the churchwarden. 'I'm sorry, vicar, but I'm not sure that I want to worship a God like that.'

'No,' said Oliver firmly, 'God has not abandoned us—though it might appear like that when we go through bad times like Greg's family are going through now. Let me go on with my story. This time it's not a Bible story in my own words, but my way of explaining how God dealt and is dealing with his self-centred people who have made such a mess of his world. Are you ready?'

'I'm all ears,' said the warden somewhat sceptically.

Oliver tried not to be put off. He hoped that his way of explaining it would get through to the group.

THE STORY OF REDEMPTION AS TOLD BY OLIVER

'One day, God looked at the beautiful world he had made, and saw a huge black cloud hanging over it. Underneath he saw smaller grey clouds around all the peoples who were warring and quarrelling with each other, and God was angry. His people had made it their world, not his, and he was heartbroken. He had made his people for love— to feel right about themselves when they loved. He had made them for joy—the joy of sharing in his creation, the joy of delighting in each other. He had made them for peace—the peace of knowing they were doing his will. Now their love was very limited, they had no permanent joy, and they did not feel at all peaceful. They did not even think they needed him any more.

'As God looked, the big cloud grew blacker and the smaller clouds grew denser. His people could no longer see him clearly even if they wanted to.

'He talked to the Word, who was with God from the beginning, part of him, but apart too, like an intimate friend, with whom he had embarked on the whole act of creation.

'"What shall we do?" asked God. "We can't just let our beloved people destroy themselves."

'There was a long pause as they remembered the time, long ago, when they had been grief-stricken by the way the world had become so corrupt, and the people had become so full of violence that they had decided to wipe them out from the face of the earth and start again with Noah (Genesis 6:5–13). Noah had faithfully loved them and obeyed them and listened to them, but it was not long before Noah's descendants had become corrupt and violent again.

'Then there was Abraham. God asked him to leave his country and people, go to the land of Canaan and start again by building up a new humanity of faith (Genesis 12:1–3), but again, it was not long before Abraham's descendants had become corrupt and violent. Then God had sent prophets—people who still listened to him and wanted to see his kingdom on earth—but not many people listened to them either.

'"My heart goes out to those few people who have always remained true to us," said the Word passionately.

'"My heart goes out to all of them," cried God with equal passion. "Especially those who have turned away from us. I can't bear to see them destroying themselves and suffering so much."

'The Word agreed. "We've got to try again. This time it must be completely different. They can't save themselves. We've got to do it for them, showing them how much we love them, and encouraging them to respond in love and accept what we have done for them."

'God took up the theme. "Somehow we've got to break up that black cloud of evil for them, get into all those clouds of sin and suffering and give people who are struggling the way to get out and into our light again."

'The light of the kingdom of God began to shine radiantly.

'The Word continued. "Somehow we must become Love in human sin, become Love in human suffering, bearing it ourselves and taking the evil out of it—by death."

'They thought about it. They thought in their humanly incomprehensible, divinely creative way, and together they had an almost heaven-and-earth-shattering thought. Then the Word spoke, slowly, sorrowfully, lovingly.

'"Let me become your Son, and be born on earth as a human being, yet still part of you, full of our grace and love and light. Then I could be Divine Love in sin, and bring forgiveness to those who turned to me. I could be Divine Love in suffering and bring our presence and healing to those who look to me. I could redeem their sin and transform their suffering." He stopped suddenly. "But I couldn't die, could I? I'm God."

'God looked at the Word in wonder and in love. "You could die as a human being physically, but I would raise you up again so that people could see you and know that you are the Son of God. And as you are raised to eternal life again, so they would be raised to new life with you with our Holy Spirit in them. And they, too, will have eternal life after their physical death."

'The light of heaven became even more radiant, then dimmed as the Word spoke again. "But not everyone would accept it. The world will still be in a mess and there will still be suffering and pain because of those who don't listen to us."

'"Yes, but those who are drawn to you in love will know your healing presence in their suffering and pain, and when they die their healing will be complete and we will all live in heavenly joy together."

'"Think of the feasts and parties we'll have," said the Word.

'"But first..." said God, and they embraced each other as Father and Son, and wept pure tears of love and sorrow. One of these tears fell through the cloud of sin on earth and was received by a young girl named Mary.'

HOW GOD HELPS US TODAY IN OUR SUFFERING

Oliver finished, and there was silence. Then Margaret broke it, struggling for the right words. 'I know—well, I know in theory that Jesus came to save us from our sins and give us eternal life—but I thought that if we try to be as good and truthful as possible, and consider other people and go to church, then we have a right to expect God's protection. But it's not quite like that, is it? You're saying that God doesn't change things. He works within the things that go wrong. It... sort of... seems a long way round... and anyway, what about the Mitchells now? They are so overwhelmed with grief, they can't see their way through it at all.'

'I know, I know,' said Oliver. 'God does not take grief away. The family have to grieve for a child who dies. They have given him birth, loved him for seven and a half years. They couldn't not grieve. But God has not abandoned them. He will help them.'

'How?' Several voices spoke at once. Oliver prayed silently for the words to convey the answer.

❖

'Well—the kind of way God may act is to send along the right people to comfort and support them in their grief, to bring his love to them in their suffering through these people. He may enable them to know that Greg is alive in spirit and may be reunited with them at their death, and he may enable them to know for themselves his comforting presence around them and in them.

'He might give them new courage to grieve purely, without bitterness, and the will, in time, to live a new life without Greg, never forgetting him but still finding purpose and joy in life again. He might help them to find love and fulfilment in their relationships with other members of their family and friends, and in doing creative things. He might encourage them to do something constructive to prevent other accidents and support other parents who have lost children.'

Oliver paused and asked hesitantly, 'Are you disappointed in the way God works?'

'I'm not sure,' said Margaret. 'I know what you're saying. After my marriage breakdown, when I was so devastated, I met Joy and her friends and they included me in their social life—which involved coming to church. I got stronger in myself because I had to survive, and after I'd built up my self-confidence again I applied for this job as Head of Hillside School. I wouldn't have had the confidence to do that when I was still married, and I do seem to be drawn toward those who are going through divorce and they seem to want to talk to me about it.'

'So you felt supported, grew stronger and started a new kind of life,' said Oliver. Margaret pulled a wry face. 'Well, yes, but it seems a pity that I had to lose my husband in order to do that!'

'It does,' agreed Oliver. 'But having lost him, it looks as if God worked in your life very effectively.'

'I suppose so. And Joy and her friends were praying for me, too.'

'That's something we can all do for the Mitchells now,' said Oliver. 'And Margaret, I know how you are suffering terribly through this tragedy, and I might not have answered all your questions, but please go on asking God for the answers. He might reveal them to you in a clearer way than I have been able to explain. We just cannot understand God fully in this life. We can only trust him—and the more we worship him, the easier it becomes to trust him. I have to leave it there.'

Margaret looked surprised. 'But Oliver, I do understand now that God does not necessarily prevent or take away the pain of tragedy, and I can see that he does somehow transform what has happened, if we turn to him. I hadn't thought of him working in such an individual, personal way. I can see too that we are more open to him after a tragedy when we feel helpless. It isn't an instant fix, though I would like it to be, and it all takes a long time—to grieve and to allow the transforming, healing process to work.'

'It does, but it's sound and it does work, believe me,' said Oliver. 'I have found for myself that God is in suffering and does help us through in ways we couldn't have imagined beforehand.'

CHECKPOINTS

- The Bible's account of creation suggests that God protected people from evil and tragedy as long as they obeyed him. But they did not always obey him. They listened to the voice of evil, and took life into their own hands. The world became corrupt.
- God did not abandon his people. He sent his Son into the world to be with people who are suffering—even when they are

disobedient to God—to deal with the power of evil himself through his death and to give new life through his Spirit. He is now with us, imperfect as we are, when we turn to him for forgiveness, and is with us when we suffer as we look to him for healing and wholeness. (For further reading, see Romans 8:1–17, 37–39; 2 Corinthians 5:21; 1 Peter 2:24.)

- Through this completely new way to bring his people back to him, God is building up a new people—a people who try to love God with all their hearts, love their neighbours as themselves and receive God's forgiveness and healing when, at times, they slip and go their own way.

Chapter 10

MOVING ON

People often ask how long the process of bereavement grief lasts, and when life will return to normal. There is no simple answer. It varies with each individual. But those who have been bereaved cannot go back to where they were before. They will have changed and their attitudes to life will have changed accordingly.

For the parents of a child who has died, the grief never ends completely. They may become more used to living with it, keeping it to themselves, and more able to cope outwardly as normal or as others expect them to be, but there will always be a place of emptiness, pain and sadness inside them.

Schools, however, have to keep to a fairly strict schedule and carry on with their routine, teaching and other activities. Children who are bereaved will usually be able to keep to this routine as long as they can stop from time to time to deal with emotions that may suddenly overwhelm them. At home they will be trying to adjust to the gap in their family life, working out how important they are now to their parents, whose entire focus seems to be on the child they have lost. They are likely to be glad to join in the normality of school life, but teachers need to be sensitive to changes in their work and behaviour for at least a year or more after the death and be ready to give them some individual attention.

Memorial services are often held some time after the funeral, when the first shock of the death is over and when people are able to recall the whole life of the person who has died, including happy memories and the things that made them laugh. They are occasions that publicly acknowledge the value of the life that has ended, and can have a healing effect on those who take part.

Fund-raising activities for a project linked to the death are usually welcomed by everyone as positive and purposeful, and can mark a 'next stage' for children outside the family. Children from within the bereaved family may not be ready to move on in their grief if the activities begin too soon after the death, but they may well be ready to move outside the restrictive and inevitably gloomy atmosphere of the home situation. Gareth was tired of his parents' protectiveness.

BREAKING OUT

Gareth thought it was his idea. His friend Mike was sure that he had thought of it first. Alan, their teacher, was convinced that he had started it off. Anyway, the idea somehow evolved in Year 6 that somewhere there should be a safe place for roller-blading and skateboarding, and if the village didn't provide one, then they would have to do something about it themselves.

Many of the children had been unnerved by Greg's accident but, as time passed, their initial fears began to subside and they wanted to be out roller-blading on the pavements again. Some of their parents, however, understandably continued to be very protective of their children, and when Gareth was searching the garage for his skateboard, his parents told him that they had taken it away.

'It's not fair,' said Gareth to Mike in the dinner queue. 'Why should I be stopped from having any fun for the rest of my life because of Greg? He always had lots of fun.'

'You could borrow my board and just not tell them,' suggested Mike brightly.

Gareth cheered up for a moment but then saddened. 'I just couldn't do it and, anyway, I know why they won't let me. I do wish there was a safe but still exciting place somewhere, where we could go on our skateboards or blades.'

'We could get them to make one in the park,' said Mike.

'Get who?' asked Gareth.

'Will you two stop talking and get a move on?' Alan interrupted their conversation and Gareth went into the dining-room, but Mike stayed put. He felt strongly about it.

'Mr Stephenson, who could we go to to get them to make a skate-park for us? Gareth's not allowed to go out on his skateboard any more and it's not fair.'

'A skate-park? For Gareth?'

'Well, for all of us really.' Mike was amazed to have his teacher's attention in a moving dinner queue. 'It'd be safe, wouldn't it? And our parents wouldn't worry about us.'

ACTION PLAN

Alan mentioned the idea of a skate-park to Margaret, who was immediately interested and suggested that Alan might encourage the boys to write a letter during literacy hour to the chairperson of the parish council. 'But I'll have a word with him first,' she added. 'George Reilly and I are old friends and he might like the idea of providing a safe place, perhaps within the existing playground area.'

'Won't it cost a lot of money?' asked Alan.

'Well, yes, but...' Margaret's face suddenly lit up. 'Why don't we raise funds for it? The whole school could be involved. It would be so constructive. I'll ring George tonight to see if it's a possibility and then I'll find out what the Mitchells think. It would be good to do something like that after the memorial service is over.'

George was very enthusiastic about the idea of a new playground specifically for roller-blading and skateboarding. He just wished he had thought of it himself. He confirmed that there was room for expansion of the existing playground and he thought that there were discretionary parish funds available for new projects. He agreed to take it to the next committee meeting.

'We could build ramps and dips and make it the best playground in the country.' George did not have to persuade his committee.

'And we must have rails too so they can do "grinds",' added one member. 'My grandson says there's nowhere here for him to practise his grinds. You should just see him doing an "ollie", though!'

The others tried to imagine it but failed.

'Er, yes...' George was temporarily silenced but quickly recovered. 'Are we all agreed that the children of this village should have whatever it takes for them to develop their skills in this important but potentially dangerous activity?' All hands were raised. 'And are we agreed that we should get on with it as soon as possible, using our own funds and then seeing how much the school raises?'

Meanwhile, Margaret was working towards the memorial service for Greg—or rather, she thought, it should be a celebration of his life. She talked it over with Oliver MacKenzie and Greg's parents, and decided that it should be held on the last afternoon of the school term, nearly three months after his death.

SERVICE TO CELEBRATE GREG'S LIFE

Now it was the last day of term, the day of the service. The children had brought bunches of wild flowers to decorate the school hall and Greg's parents had offered their favourite photograph of him in his football kit to stand on the platform table with their flowers. At the back of the platform was a large collage of Christ against a background of heaven and the world, which Abby and other members of Greg's class had made, and on the walls around there were other children's pictures.

Frances began to play Schumann's *Scenes from Childhood* as the children were filing in to sit on the floor at the front. Adults came in at the back, greeted by children from Year 6 with a service sheet. When the seats were all taken, people were still coming, so room had to be made for them at the back and even outside the open doors. The music stopped as Margaret and Oliver walked on to the platform.

Margaret tried to smile round at everyone. 'Welcome to Hillside School. It's been a very sad term for all of us, but the children and staff still wanted to do something to celebrate the life of Greg. As you can see on the walls around us, there are pictures and poems and writing by the children, which are their attempts to express something of the fun of knowing Greg. We hope you will all find something in the service to thank God for as we remember Greg in his short but very full and quite unforgettable life. We'll start by singing a hymn which many of you will have sung as children, "Jesus bids us shine".'

After the hymn, Oliver asked everyone to sit. 'I know you children have asked a lot of questions this term about heaven—and you are not the only ones. Jesus' friends asked him a question about heaven. They asked him who was the most important person there. I think they hoped that they might become the most important people there. But Jesus didn't answer in the way they wanted. Do you remember what he did? He held out his hand to a child and asked her to come and stand by him. Then he put his arm round her in front of everyone and said to the grown-ups, "If you don't change and become like a child, you will never get into the kingdom of heaven. But if you are as humble..." (that means don't think you are important) "... as this child, you are the greatest in the kingdom of heaven" (Matthew 18:1–4).

'Let us pray. Heavenly Father, we thank you for our children. Today we want to thank you especially for the life of Greg Mitchell. Give us the grace to be thankful even in our sadness. We ask this through Jesus Christ, who loves all children, and has a special place for them in heaven. Amen.'

As people raised their heads again, Margaret held up a book for everyone to see. 'I'm going to ask Gareth and Ellie to come up here now and present this "memory book" to their parents. It has contributions from children and staff here, and also from Greg's Sunday school, the Beavers and his all-important football club. It is an attempt to capture the essence of Greg's life by those who knew him. Neil and Sue, please accept this with all our love.'

Gareth and Ellie went up to the platform, holding hands tightly, took the book from Margaret and carefully carried it back to their parents, who had been prepared beforehand and were able to receive it with composure.

'Now Ellie's class would like to act out for you a song which has helped them to understand a bit more about the process of life and death, and life beyond death. It's all about a growing caterpillar.'

Frances played the tune through as Lorraine brought the Foundation class up and carefully spread out a green blanket on the floor of the platform. Some of the children lay down on it and lifted their heads up and down, pretending to be caterpillars eating, while the rest of the class sang:

Caterpillar, caterpillar, munching, munching, ate through a leaf or two,
For caterpillar, caterpillar, munching, munching, didn't have a lot to do.
But the leaves were very tasty, and there seemed a lot to spare,
So caterpillar, caterpillar went on munching, munching everywhere.

During the next verse Lorraine covered them up with a green sheet.

Caterpillar, caterpillar, feeling sleepy, fixed up a silken bed.
Then caterpillar, caterpillar climbed inside and covered up his sleepy head.
In the dark he slept and rested as the days and nights went by,
Till on a sunny morning when the silk bed burst, he was a butterfly!

Lorraine whipped off the sheet and the children all sprang up with raised arms like wings. Then slowly they began to shake and spread out their arms and fly round the platform.

Butterfly, oh butterfly, a-flitt'ring, flutt'ring; oh what a sight to see.
And as the lovely butterfly was flutt'ring by, I heard him sing a song to me:
'Oh I never knew God could do such a wondrous thing for me;
for he took me as a caterpillar and he made a butterfly of me.'

The last two lines were sung loudly and clearly by Hollie as the others fluttered off the platform and went back to their chairs, followed by the singers and then by Hollie.

'Thank you, children,' said Margaret. 'You did that beautifully.' She looked round at the adults. 'Since Greg died, we've all tried to face the subject of death—what happens, and how it leaves the rest of us feeling for a very long time. I hope we all understand it a little bit better after that drama. Now I'm going to say a few words about Greg, beginning with his first day at school when his parents said, "This one is quite different from Gareth. I hope he doesn't lead you too much of a dance."'

Margaret paused and smiled. 'Actually, "dance" is the word that seems particularly apt to describe Greg's time at Hillside...'

She went on to give a lively, entertaining account of Greg's life and finished by saying, 'I hope I have managed to convey to you something of the joy of his character, his gifts, some of his weaknesses, and the place he has held in the school and will always hold in the hearts of those of us who knew him well. Will the school choir now lead us into prayer.'

Frances gave a note and the choir sang unaccompanied.

Give me peace, O Lord, I pray,
In my work and in my play;
And inside my heart and mind,
Lord, give me peace.

Give peace to the world, I pray,
Let all quarrels cease today.
May we spread your light and love:
Lord, give us peace.

Four children from Greg's class stood and read out their own prayers.

'Dear God, thank you for Greg. He was nearly always kind and made us laugh a lot. Amen.'

'O God, thank you for making Greg. He was like a bright star in our class. Amen.'

'Jesus, I am very sad because Greg died and he was my favourite person. He liked everyone and was different from anyone else. Amen.'

'Please, God, look after Greg in your heavenly home and give him everything he wants. And please look after Greg's mum and dad and sister and brother. Amen.'

Carole, their teacher, went up to stand with the four children. 'This is a poem which Greg's parents asked me to read. It expresses how they sometimes think about Greg now. It's called "Learning to Fly", by Adrian Plass.

> *We have stretched our arms towards him.*
> *We have longed to draw him down,*
> *Sought to raise him from the frozen heart of stone,*
> *We have searched the rocky passes with our sisters and our brothers,*
> *We have raced through shadowed valleys of our own.*
> *And our fingertips have touched him,*
> *Yes, our fingertips have touched him,*
> *Though we move before his touch can slow us down,*
> *How we grieve that in our turning,*
> *The eternal moment passes,*
> *As our newly floating hopes begin to drown.*
> *And we long for when we rise with him,*
> *Beyond this place of searching,*
> *Moving effortlessly through the new-made sky,*
> *Where the blue could not be deeper,*
> *And a child's sun is smiling,*
> *On the citizens of heaven as they fly.*
> *Then the rising will not lift us, nor the falling bring us down,*
> *And the springs will ring with echoing delight,*
> *But until we spread our wings in the company of angels,*
> *Dancing is the nearest thing to flight.*

There was a silence in the hall while Carole and the children returned to their places. Margaret said quietly, 'Our service will end with a hymn about the dance of life—"Lord of the Dance".'

The children's voices rang out above all the adults' in the last lines of the hymn.

> *I am the life that'll never, never die.*
> *I'll live in you if you live in me,*
> *I am the Lord of the Dance, said he.*
>
> (SYDNEY CARTER)

They all remained standing as Oliver came forward with hands uplifted to say a blessing.

'The Lord bless you and watch over you. The Lord make his face to shine upon you and be gracious to you. The Lord give you his peace. Go then, in peace, and the God of all peace go with you.'

FUND-RAISING

As the summer term came round, the children were encouraged to think about ideas for fund-raising for a new playground specifically for users of roller-blades and skateboards. Most of the parents, including Greg's, were keen on the idea of a safe play area for their children, and some of them volunteered to be involved in fund-raising. It was something positive that they could do.

The school had had to return almost to normal after Greg's death and, for some reason that Margaret could not quite identify, Greg's name was no longer part of the children's everyday conversation. Perhaps they did not want to cope with the pain and sadness it brought. But now, as every class talked about what they would like to do to raise money, his name came up easily in conversations again and a new energy entered into their thinking about Greg.

By far the most popular idea among the children was a non-school uniform day, with 50 pence to pay for the privilege of coming to school in clothes of their own choice. A school disco came second, especially as Greg had been such a star at the last disco. Frances offered to put on a concert with the choir and music group and suggested that it might take place in the village hall one evening. Abby's parents volunteered to organize a sponsored school hike.

Greg's class wanted to do something on their own. They talked and laughed about the kind of things Greg would have suggested—mostly involving food—and in the end Carole had to move them on. 'Why don't we make cakes and fruit punch and sell them at the concert? We could use the kitchen on Wednesday afternoons after school, and I'll keep what we bake in my freezer.'

The fund-raising activities were about more than the money they raised. They marked the beginning of a way forward for the school, a sense of common purpose, and a feeling that some good, however small, was emerging out of the tragedy of Greg's death that had affected them all—and it was fun. It gave the children permission to smile when they talked about Greg.

Of all the fund-raising activities, the sponsored hike was a particular success. After the concert in the village hall, the community as a whole became involved in the project and everyone seemed keen to sponsor someone. All the Mitchell family joined in the hike, with Ellie sometimes walking with her parents when she was tired and sometimes running ahead with other children. Ellie seemed to have grown up from being a little child into a schoolgirl, but she still had what Lorraine, her teacher, called 'Ellie's bad days' when she would suddenly withdraw or have bursts of temper or tears, or did not want to mix with the others in the playground. She never talked much about her feelings but was always responsive to individual attention and warmth from Joan, the classroom assistant.

Gareth seemed all right on the surface, but Alan tried to be alert to his 'quiet times' when he did not seem able to concentrate on his work. He had fallen behind the rest of the class in his general development and seemed to prefer the company of Mike or one or two other close friends. On the whole, Alan thought Gareth was doing all right, though he never looked very happy.

THE NEW SKATE-PARK

Then, something happened that made Gareth really happy. He was playing with his model aeroplane in his bedroom one evening when there was a knock on the door, and his parents called him down. Mr Reilly from the council was standing in the hall and said he would like a word with Gareth.

'You know the new skate-park we are building,' began George. Gareth nodded. He knew the playground all right, but what was the point when he hadn't got a skateboard any more? 'Well,' said George importantly, 'it's being opened next week and I would like you to be the first one to go on it with your skateboard. Would you do that?'

Gareth looked at his parents. 'It's all right, we've agreed,' said his father gently. 'You can have your skateboard back. We'd like you to do what Mr Reilly is asking, but only if you want to.'

'Really? I can go on my skateboard again?' Gareth felt it was the best thing that had happened to him since everything changed on the day Greg died.

'What about me?' said Ellie, who had suddenly appeared at Gareth's side. 'I've got a new pink two-wheeler bike.'

'With stabilisers,' added Gareth.

'I can nearly ride it without stabilisers, can't I, Mum?'

'Well... nearly,' said Sue. 'We must take your bike when we go to watch Gareth skateboard again.'

THE DANCE GOES ON

George stood at the entrance to the new playground with Gareth at his side and spoke in a loud voice to the crowd of schoolchildren, staff, councillors and other members of the village community who had gathered in the park for the occasion. 'This skate-park has been built in memory of Greg Mitchell. I am now going to ask his brother Gareth to open it.' He handed a large pair of scissors to Gareth, who cut the ribbon, then went forward with his skateboard and did a running jump on to it.

Everyone watched as Gareth moved—a little unsteadily at first, but then, with a new surge of energy, faster and faster, over a ramp, on and off the grind bar, jumping in the air, and round again. For a fleeting, eternal moment, heaven and earth came together as Greg seemed to be speeding alongside him, full of laughter and fun.

Margaret thought she heard the echo of his laughter and remembered the words of the poem read at the memorial service.

> *But until we spread our wings in the company of angels,*
> *Dancing is the nearest thing to flight.*

The worst had happened. A child had died. But the dance of the children would go on, and in time, when they were ready, adults would join in too.

POEMS AND SONGS

'Caterpillar, caterpillar' by Susan Sayers. Arr. Andrew Moore. *Complete Anglican Hymns Old and New* No. 782.

'Give me peace, O Lord', by Estelle White. Arr. Andrew Moore. *Complete Anglican Hymns Old and New* No. 802.

'Lord of the Dance', by Sydney Carter. Arr. Noel Rawsthorne. *Complete Anglican Hymns Old and New* No. 305.

'Learning to Fly', by Adrian Plass, from the book *Learning to Fly* (OM Publications, 1996)

SUGGESTED FURTHER READING

FOR ADULTS TO READ TO CHILDREN

Grandad's Prayers of the Earth by Douglas Wood, Walker Books Ltd, 1999
For 5–7 year olds. Not specifically Christian.

Goodbye Pappa by Una Leary, Orchard Books, 1999
Picture book for 5–6 year olds.

I Miss You by Pat Thomas, Hodder Wayland, 2001
For 5–7 year olds. Good explanations for the child.

Badger's Parting Gifts by Susan Varley, Collins Picture Books, 2002
For 5–8 year olds.

Talking about Death by Earl A. Grollman, Beacon Press, Boston, 1983
A dialogue between parent and child, for 5–7 year olds.

A Dragon in Your Heart by Sophie LeBlanc, Jessica Kingsley, 1999
For 6–7 year olds. Explains hospital treatment for mother who has cancer.

Waterbugs and Dragonflies by Doris Stickney, Continuum, 2002
For 4–8 year olds. Gives a concept of death and resurrection.

FOR OLDER CHILDREN

Let's Talk About… When a Parent Dies by Elizabeth Weitzman, Heinemann Library, 1997
For 8–11 year olds to read themselves, about a father dying.

FOR ADULTS, PARTICULARLY TEACHERS

Helping Children to Manage Loss by Brenda Mallon, Jessica Kingsley, 1998

The Forgotten Mourners by Susan C. Smith, Jessica Kingsley, 1999

Children and Bereavement, Death and Loss. What Can the School Do? by Patsy Wagner, produced by the National Association for Pastoral Care in Education, 1993

★★★ ALSO FROM BRF ★★★

Children need to explore topical and often sensitive issues in a safe environment with adults they know and trust. These three books by Heather Butler are designed to address a range of topical and often sensitive issues relevant to the lives of children aged 6–10. They can be used on a one-to-one basis with the individual child, in a group or with a whole class, particularly during Circle Time or PSHE.

STORIES TO MAKE YOU THINK
ISBN 1 84101 034 0 £3.99
Topics covered include bereavement, family issues, spirituality, self-value, bullying, racial issues, gender issues and making friends.

MORE STORIES TO MAKE YOU THINK
ISBN 1 84101 141 X £4.99
Topics covered include redundancy, abuse, bereavement, Third World issues, boredom, honesty, anger, personal hygiene and serious illness.

FURTHER STORIES TO MAKE YOU THINK
(available July 2004)
ISBN 1 84101 202 5 £4.99
Topics covered include fairness, making mistakes, setting simple goals, looking after living things, cultural differences, democracy, media, peer pressure, teasing and bullying, stereotypes, behaving responsibly, stranger danger and living with separated parents.

To order, please use the form opposite.

ORDER FORM

REF	TITLE	PRICE	QTY	TOTAL
034 0	*Stories to Make You Think*	£3.99		
141 X	*More Stories to Make You Think*	£4.99		
202 5	*Further Stories to Make You Think*	£4.99		

POSTAGE AND PACKING CHARGES					Postage and packing:	
order value	UK	Europe	Surface	Air Mail	Donation:	
£7.00 & under	£1.25	£3.00	£3.50	£5.50	**Total enclosed:**	
£7.01–£30.00	£2.25	£5.50	£6.50	£10.00		
Over £30.00	free	prices on request				

Name _____ Account Number _____

Address_____

_____ Postcode _____

Telephone Number _____ Email _____

Payment by: Cheque ❏ Mastercard ❏ Visa ❏ Postal Order ❏ Switch ❏

Credit card no. ☐☐☐☐ ☐☐☐☐ ☐☐☐☐ ☐☐☐☐   Expires ☐☐ ☐☐

Switch card no. ☐☐☐☐☐☐☐☐☐☐☐☐☐☐☐☐☐☐

Issue no. of Switch card ☐☐☐☐   Expires ☐☐ ☐☐

Signature _____ Date _____

All orders must be accompanied by the appropriate payment.

Please send your completed order form to:
BRF, First Floor, Elsfield Hall, 15–17 Elsfield Way, Oxford OX2 8FG
Tel. 01865 319700 / Fax. 01865 319701 Email: enquiries@brf.org.uk

❏ Please send me further information about BRF publications.

Available from your local Christian bookshop.   BRF is a Registered Charity

🌿 barnabas

Resourcing children's work in church and school

Simply go to
www.brf.org.uk
and visit the
barnabas pages

BRF is a Registered Charity

A Browse our books and buy online in our **bookshop**.

B In the **forum**, join discussions with friends and experts in children's work. Chat through the problems we all face, issues facing children's workers, where-do-I-find… questions and more.

C **Free** easy-to-use downloadable **ideas** for children's workers and teachers. Ideas include:
- Getting going with prayer
- Getting going with drama
- Getting going with the Bible… and much more!

D In **The Big Picture**, you'll find short fun reports on Barnabas training events, days we've spent in schools and churches, as well as expertise from our authors, and other useful articles.

E In the section on **Godly Play**, you'll find a general introduction and ideas on how to get started with this exciting new approach to Christian education.